S0-DYE-424

DISCARDED

44　　　　　PORTF

TAKING CARE OF YOURSELF IS PRODUCTIVE

TAKE THE RISK

loved the plan
ntil I met the
ream

Praise for *Happily Grey*

"I have had the pleasure of knowing Mary Lawless Lee over the past several years. She is the definition of the modern superwoman who embodies the characteristics that have garnered respect and admiration from all who follow her. Mary is so very kind, incredibly smart, humble, and hardworking. She is an incredibly devoted mother, wife, and entrepreneur, and I am so excited that she is sharing her honest personal journey with everyone. I cannot wait to see what she does next, as I am sure the best is yet to come."

Rachel Zoe, co-CEO and founder of Rachel Zoe, Inc.,
Curateur, Rachel Zoe Collection, and The Zoe Report;
chairwoman of Rachel Zoe Ventures

"*Happily Grey* is a love letter to one's inner child. I've known Mary for several years, and seeing her pull back the curtain and share these honest, vulnerable experiences is an inspiration and guide to us all. From her struggles through motherhood, launching and running multiple businesses, navigating the boundaries of social media, and her hard-won moments of success, Mary delivers heartfelt words on her discovery back to that childlike wonder and joy she once knew."

Jen Atkin, founder of OUAI and Mane Addicts,
celebrity hairstylist, and author of *Blowing My Way to the Top*

"From someone we know well for her signature style comes a remarkably personal memoir about motherhood, womanhood, and everything in between. Mary shows us that it's okay to not be okay and shares how to navigate the struggles women face in motherhood, business, and relationships. From the colorful design to the heartfelt advice, *Happily Grey* is for anyone striving to craft a perfectly imperfect life."

Clea Shearer, coauthor of *The Home Edit* and
costar of the Netflix series *Get Organized with The Home Edit*

"Timely, important, and vulnerable is Mary Lawless Lee's message and road map for anyone seeking deeper understanding, clarity, healing, and happiness. Mary's gift as a storyteller is fully displayed in this courageous and intimate memoir. With every page, she reminds us of the importance of owning and sharing our stories. Mary's pursuit of living a wholehearted life is inspiring, and this book can encourage you to do the same."

Miles Adcox, proprietor and chairman, Onsite Wellness Group; founder, Human School; cofounder, The Oaks

"As a friend, a fellow mother, and someone who has been able to watch Mary's career as a content creator grow into multiple successful businesses, it's an absolute delight and inspiration to read through these pages that perfectly capture the drive, dedication, and passion Mary puts into everything she does. *Happily Grey* is anything but a highlight reel. Mary vulnerably shares her life lessons and gives us an inspiring guide to stay curious and rediscover that childlike wonder."

Amber Venz Box, cofounder and president, LTK

"In this book, Mary shows fellow women and mothers that while we may not be able to have it all, we can have so much more if we're willing to look inside ourselves and find the courage to change. If you're ready to crack open your heart, show the world who you really are, and lead your life on your terms, this book is for you!"

Julie Solomon, influencer marketing coach, bestselling author, and host of *The Influencer Podcast*

happily
grey

happily
grey

Stories, Souvenirs, and Everyday
Wonders from the Life In Between

MARY LAWLESS LEE

WITH SHANNON LEE MILLER

HARPER HORIZON

Published by Harper Horizon, an imprint of HarperCollins Focus LLC.

Any internet addresses, phone numbers, or company or product information printed in this book are offered as a resource and are not intended in any way to be or to imply an endorsement by Harper Horizon, nor does Harper Horizon vouch for the existence, content, or services of these sites, phone numbers, companies, or products beyond the life of this book.

The information in this book has been carefully researched by the author and is intended to be a source of information only. Readers are urged to consult with their physicians or other professional advisors to address specific medical or other issues. The author and the publisher assume no responsibility for any injuries suffered or damages incurred during or as a result of the use or application of the information contained herein.

ISBN 978-0-7852-9313-2 (Ebook)
ISBN 978-0-7852-9312-5 (HC)

Library of Congress Control Number: 2022930134

Printed in Canada

22 23 24 25 26 TC 10 9 8 7 6 5 4 3 2 1

For my family:

Mad, Navy, Indie, and *you*, the wonderful community that for years has wrapped
me up in love, celebrated my good days, mourned my bad ones, and stood
alongside me on all the days in between. Not everybody gets to grow up with a
direct line to honesty, encouragement, and inspiration. Thank you for growing
with me, for giving me a chance, and for making my world so damn beautiful.

PS: Madison Lee, none of this would be possible without you. When I fell
in love with you, I fell in love with life. You are the greatest gift.

Contents

Author's Note

I get a lot of questions.

    "What facial serum do you use?"

    "How did you deal with your baby's reflux?"

    "Should I wear gold or mustard to my sister's fall wedding?"

    "Where did you get that sweater?"

    "What does *Happily Grey* mean?"

That last question comes up more often than any other, and every time it's posed, I struggle to put the answer into words. My deepest hope is that this book will (finally) do just that.

Grey isn't the last name of my first husband or the town where I grew up. It's not my favorite kind of weather or an ode to any long-running, major network medical drama. I promise, *Happily Grey* is not some humorless monochromatic fashion statement. If anything, it's all about color.

I grew up in a world where everything seemed to be black or white, right or wrong, true or untrue, but I found myself, and learned to love myself, in the spaces between. In the grey areas I found relief. Thank God it wasn't all black and white. The discovery that it was safe for me to create my own way, to be undecided, to make my own rules, allowed me to step into my freedom and changed my life completely. *Happily Grey* is about the bliss of uncertainty, the thrill of curiosity, the beautiful, electrifying, intense experience of wonder. It's about things that, by nature, are hard to put into words. Friends, it's all about asking questions, so please, keep asking them.

In these pages, we'll step back together into the times and places that have lovingly and (very, very) patiently shaped me, reliving moments when a world that seemed small and simple revealed itself as impossibly vast and complex, sending me onward with lessons, memories, and keepsakes to share. There are photographs, narratives, and recipes, tips for doing your hair and for surviving your divorce. Consider it my philosophical travel guide . . . from the girl who boarded her first flight at the age of twenty.

Re-creating these stories and scenes has been magical and emotional and imperfect and often very, very silly. Some memories were clear, and others were hazy. Some names are real, others are not. The heart of every person and place, though, has been thoughtfully and reverently preserved. I am deeply thankful to every human being, blue sky, and glimpse of beauty that has been a part of my journey, stopping me in my tracks, guiding me, and helping me to open my eyes a little wider. Also, I'm thankful to you. My greatest, deepest hope is that you find pieces of yourself in these stories, that you'll remember the feel of dirt on your own bare toes and the very first days of falling in love. I hope that you'll know, without a single doubt, that you're not alone in the wildness, woe, and wonder of this world.

Love,

Mary Lawless Lee

CHAPTER 1

White Lilies

*Keep your eyes wide open—there's so much
more to see than what you're looking for.*

Marshall, Texas, is famous for pottery, fire ants, and a courthouse too large and imposing to watch over a city where surprise hardly lives, let alone trouble. Since 1865 it's been the largest manufacturer of red-clay planters in America, and there is more gingham per capita here than anywhere else on earth. At least, it seems that way to me.

For years my family has raised cattle down on FM 2199. They're enormous, gentle creatures with doe eyes and wet noses who mostly ignore my brother, John, and I, and instead spend all day moaning to the hot sun the way coyotes call to the moon. We like them well enough but prefer to climb up onto the round hay bales next to their pasture and race each other back and forth across the tops of the giant wheels, leaping between them as far and fast as our legs can muster, hoping we don't fall seven feet down to the dirt. When we run out of steam, we just sit next to each other watching the cows walk back and forth as one big black mass, sometimes making a horrible game of guessing how soon the trailer will gather them for slaughter. Kids in Texas don't get sad about cows becoming steak; they get

hungry. And kids in Texas get hungry a lot—as soon as you're old enough to throw a ball, you're on a sports team.

Dad is mostly in logging now and Mom is a teacher, but our home is a true ranch home: a calico collection of brownish bricks and brown shag sandwiched between two of my grandfather's Holstein-Brahman herds. It's good here and we know it, even as kids. We don't long for some Narnia or enchanted forest when we have five hundred acres of pasture and creek and pond, when we're too young to know time and live instead in a forever golden hour of big skies, bare toes, and family. We know the world is bigger than Marshall. We know about Little Rock and Shreveport, that Grandpa fought in Europe, and that they sent men to the moon, but parts of us refuse to believe any of it. We believe that you should leave the house as soon as you finish your breakfast and spend your day listening to the sound the berry branches make when they bow across the switchgrass. The world beyond us may be big, but I can't be convinced that it holds more freedom.

At nine and eight years old respectively, John and I decide we might become fishermen. We like fishing because Dad likes it and because our older sisters have moved on to other things like blue eyeshadow and Pearl Jam. In the evenings after dinner, we peek into the wall of hardbacked books and field guides that is our father's office and find him examining lures under his desk lamp and trawling the classifieds for the absolute perfect boat. His brow, an accordion of joy and frustration, contracts and releases as he reads the local newspaper, considering first a little skiff, then something sturdier for the whole family.

John and I are captivated by his deep, quiet, mysterious love for the sport and do our best to try it on for ourselves, imagining the weight of a bass on the line or the muscle of a mean catfish dragged up from deep in the sludge. We can't quite figure out how we'll structure our business. John is sixteen months older than I am, so he'll probably have to run the ranch when he's grown. I'm planning to have at least ten babies, and we both know there's no way they'll all fit in the johnboat with me. But we're still determined. We decide that for now, we should start by practicing the fishing part.

Summer is an immersion in a new language: jigs and spoons, swim baits and poppers, stickworms and stinger hooks. We wake before the mile-wide sun and, rubbing our still-swollen eyes, trudge down to the pond's edge to catch the bass while they're still half asleep like we are. We choose the pond closest to the house at first, just in case our lines get caught in a gum tree or Mom hollers for us to come finish our workbook assignment. She always

makes us do math and writing during the summer. We don't like it at all, but she promises we'll thank her later and neither of us have the gall to argue with the Teacher of the Year about learning. Even though she'd never say it herself, it's true. At only forty years old, she's by far the best teacher in the school, the district, and the state. Maybe the whole world.

Besides, I want to do well. Even at eight years old, it matters to me. I want to get good grades, be a good cheerleader, and score home runs with my softball team, the Wild Things. Some of the kids just stare up at the clouds, but I want to win.

The pond water is opaque and colored rust like the dirt beneath our feet. It gives none of its secrets away except for the occasional, always electrifying bubble. John does better at fishing than I do, and I hate it in secret. He shows off, pulling in a little brim that resigns quickly to the reality of the hook and nearly forgives his clumsy ten-year-old fingers for tearing its lips. I stand jealously aside as he goes through motions of sizing it up and tossing it back into the murk. Occasionally, after hours of patient prayer and holding my bladder, I'll catch something small, simultaneously rejoicing in it and wishing it was mighty. Our favorite, most serious excursions come when Dad takes one of us with him to Caddo Lake where the white bass live. I'm just nine when it's my turn.

He wakes me early in July and Mom has bacon, eggs, and buttered toast waiting for us.

She never lets any of us miss a meal; even if we left at midnight she'd find a way to fill our bellies before sending us off for the day. The kitchen, like the rest of the house, is already spotless, as though breakfast just appeared from thin air.

"Have fun," Mom smiles, retreating to the living room to clean an invisible mess.

Dad and I eat quickly and mostly in silence. Then we head out to the truck and drive off into the early pink sky, with the Ranger (his boat of the moment) trailing faithfully behind us down the road.

Dad drives the speed limit, never faster, with hands at ten and two and eyes fixed far out onto the horizon. He likes music but we rarely turn the radio on. His taste is specific, but everything he likes, I like too. On Sundays he sings "Oh! Darling" by the Beatles to irritate Mom when she's trying to do her makeup for church, and if the weather and his mood are both in the right place, he'll roll down the truck windows sometimes and blare "I'll Drown in My Tears" by Johnny Winter. We'll sing every sad word at the top of our lungs.

We don't talk very much, but Dad and I are both content to stay busy in our heads. I like looking across the wide bench seat and imagining what he's thinking, wondering if he's quietly plotting out the places that will be best for us to cast our lines like some kind of Texan fishing mystic, or if he's worried about work. Wondering about him is even better than knowing some days. Every ten miles or so I'll ask him what we packed for lunch or if I can drive the boat, just so that he knows I'm excited. He'll answer me back in the quiet, articulate voice, lovingly crafted and insisted upon by his English-teacher mother. Unless he's mad or Johnny Winter is on, he never raises his voice.

The sun rises proudly as we turn onto the highway, and I squint, little bits of glimmering light draped over my lashes. Through the haze, I catch our reflections side by side in the windshield and can't tell whose gangly, wading bird legs belong to whom. I'm starting to look like him. The regular jeans Mom buys aren't long enough in the inseam or small enough in the waist. My wide white teeth wrestle one another for space in my mouth, which forces me to smile almost all the time. I'm awkward and I know it, but I look into him as if he were a mirror and know that eventually, it'll all even out. I'll have copper skin that knows the sun so well it doesn't bother to fade. Long dunes of muscle will surround the knobbly knees and sharp elbows, and I won't be quite so good at scaring the blackbirds who steal from the vegetable garden. We roll along toward the state border, to the place where our Texas wetland becomes a Louisiana bayou, and I think about what it will feel like to grow older. All I really know is that I want to be successful, I want to be beautiful, I want to be perfect. I want to make my family proud. If I keep focusing, studying, fishing, and praying, I know that I will.

The truck is happier when the asphalt gives way to gravel. We are too. It means we're getting close. Silver flashes of lake water peek through the cypress groves and the gas stations stop advertising fuel and tempt us only with their bait and breakfast. After forty-five minutes of driving, my skin has finally absorbed the thick layer of sunscreen that my mom painted on and my limbs have gotten achy and restless.

Deep breaths of algae, the half-full gas can, and the few but fragrant pines fill my chest and I ready myself for the adventure, shutting my eyes, trying to feel the potbellied, shimmering fish tugging at my shoulders, fighting and twisting on my line. I remind myself that I'm tall for my age and stronger than I look. They call me Mercules at school because I once beat every boy in my class in a cafeteria arm-wrestling tournament. Mom teaches my fourth-grade class and normally wouldn't stand for any kind of horseplay or strongman carnival games. This time, though, she pretended not to see and watched me take down Chance West from the corner of her eye.

The truck hits a divot in the road, and I lurch forward toward the dash feeling small

and timid all over again. Once more the road changes, this time from gravel to red dust, and Dad backs the truck toward a place so empty and perfect for launching a boat that it must be a secret that belongs only to him.

Caddo Lake is still a wild place. You wouldn't insult it by attempting to swim there. The water is an uninviting black-brown-green slurry that looks like patent leather from the shore. In some spots, it smells like the end of the world: carcass, rotten wood, and standing water. In others, it's like the beginning: just-bloomed honeysuckle, Christmas fern, hints of ocean that have traveled two hundred miles upstream. Nearly everything in nature seems to live here—osprey nest in the tall trees, snuffling hogs swish their tails in the brush, fat nutrias waddle up the banks and swim like rat-sharks in the shallows. There are even alligators that silently float alongside the hunks of dead wood and remind me of my grandma's fancy handbags. Every year, dozens of people swear that they see Bigfoot marching through the bayou, but we haven't seen him—not yet anyway. If he did show up at the tree line, I wouldn't even notice. My attention is pinned on the one and only mission: big fish, not Bigfoot.

As we push off, a flash of rain washes us. The sunscreen that sunk into my skin re-appears in milky tributaries flowing down to my wrists and slapping the tin belly of the boat. The torrent lasts about a minute before the sun comes out and the clouds shrink away. Dad putters around our cove and I take it in. Steam rises from the tree bark and the full bells of the trumpet flowers spill out onto one another. Our clothes are wet, but it isn't a bother to us. Dad says that we're lucky—the fish seem to like it best after a rainfall. He throws his line into the waterweeds and hooks a largemouth bass almost immediately to prove it. I furrow my brow and cast my own long, elegant line after his and wait for more than an hour. Eventually, I get a small chain pickerel he helps me reel in, and later, a young bass I bring up onto the boat all by myself, which Dad's ecstatic over. I smile at him as he takes a measuring tape to the small, shimmering body and let him congratulate me, but I want the trophy fish, the one nobody will ever believe existed. I refocus, expertly slipping bait onto my hook, paying no mind to worm guts under my fingernails.

The sun has passed over the middle of the sky when Dad decides it's time to come in. He hooked a bass he guesses is six pounds and an enormous catfish that fought like a lion, pulling the Ranger onto its side and making him sweat through his T-shirt. He hates catfish, but he's always proud when he brings one in.

"It was a good day," he decides out loud, pulling the motor to a sputter and then letting it drift. I rest my chin on the hot aluminum lip of the boat and look down into the water, which is dreary and brown.

Afternoon breeze sends a shiver across the water's surface and just for a moment, the muck clears. A perfect white lily looks up at me. Her petals, pristine as clean linen, fan out boldly into the brackish water, somehow repelling the mud that covers everything else. Yellow filaments burst from her middle and she's so beautiful, I hardly notice the perfect heart-shaped leaf that anchors her. I count the petals in my mind. *1, 2, 3, 4, 5 . . . 11 . . . 17,* and lose my way quickly. I lose everything quickly—the thoughts of fish, rods, reels, and Bassmaster trophies. I'm too wonderstruck to do anything but take in what I can of the miraculous flower hiding in the filth. As we float over it and away, I think for a moment that I should have pulled her in like the pickerel, but then the sweetest, truest peace rolls over me and I realize that I already have. I'm no longer looking for the perfect, gleaming bass but at everything that lives around him. In an instant, an empty lake fills with miracles.

My spine tingles the whole way back to the rocks, and goose bumps rise on my arms even though it's ninety degrees under the big, bearded oaks. I reel in the wide veiny leaves suspended over the lake water by long invisible strands of spider silk. I watch them catch the sun in their skins and cast the branches beneath in bronze. I capture the water moccasin moving slowly, far off on the surface, body covered in black shimmering petals of its own. I bring in my father's love, the drone of the katydids, and the way the sun stares down at its own reflection in the water. I am, for the first time, an expert at fishing. The bow of the Ranger kisses the shore and the lily appears in my mind once more, as though to remind me, *Keep your eyes wide open—there's so much more to see than what you're looking for.*

Combing through the matted undergrowth of adolescence, I clutch the white lily and hold her close to my chest. When the world seems small, I try my best to peek at it through her parted white segments and remember the secret universe under the water, in the forest, and beyond the place where the sun dips. For a few years more, John and I rip through pastures with our rods and reels, both of us playing Peter Pan, though as I get older, I show up more often dressed as Wendy (but with a plastic stroller and seven baby dolls).

At twelve and thirteen, we splash less in the creek and instead hurl our tucked-up selves into the ear-shaped swimming pool Mom and Dad put out back. Our bodies change. We make new friends. John wakes up a driver one day and I wake up a cheerleader. Neither of us loses our taste for wading in the pond water, even when the tips of our hair go green from the pool's chlorine, but we have brand-new hungers that guide us. We stop talking about the fishing company. The sky still hangs persistently gold over the farm. I imagine that it always will, but the truth remains that I take my rod down to the pond less at seventeen than I did at nine. Even so, I cast my line and my eyes outward, never knowing or wanting to know what may come back to me. Or at least, I try.

Keep SAKES

White Lilies

There is nothing from childhood that I don't hold close. I might know how to navigate the New York subway system, but I also know how to bait a hook. I can wear heels all day on a shoot, but only because my feet are tough from wading at the edge of the pond in too-big rubber boots. I know what to order at the French Laundry, and—from years of driving to Dallas for fast-pitch tournaments—I know what to order at Applebee's too. The world shapes me, but East Texas made me. It was where I had my very first taste of curiosity *and* of brisket. It was weekend games, joining the team, belonging.

I went to church every Sunday looking for God but found him just as easily in the still waters of Caddo Lake and in my dad's singing voice. I'm proud to be from a small town that, by virtue of its simplicity, taught me to look deeper, reach farther, and keep my eyes wide open. It gave me the gift of wonder, and it also gave me the ability to make a pair of jean shorts in less than ten minutes.

*Keep your eyes wide open.
There's so much more to see
than what you're looking for.*

Fishing *(for Inner Peace)*

Hardly anybody talks about it, but fishing is basically yoga for the rugged outdoorsman. Long before I lifted my hips into downward-facing dog or fell over in a packed studio trying to be a humble warrior (which was, you guessed it, incredibly humbling), I practiced mindfulness with a bucket of brown worms, my trusty blue Zebco rod, and a pond full of murky brown water. Fishing is about stillness, listening, looking, and staying present. And if you're with my dad, there are absolutely no screens allowed—unless you catch something worth bragging about. Let's go fish!

STEPS:

1. Before things get too "reel," you've got to get your license. Don't worry, there's no bass-identification exam. You don't need an advanced knowledge of freshwater ecosystem dynamics. All you need to do is hop online, find your state's wildlife resource agency, fill out an application, and pay a small fee. If you're not fishing on public property, you can skip this step. Just make sure you ask permission from the property owners. I'm looking at you, John.

2. Gear up! I have it on good authority that you can walk into a Bass Pro Shop with a wide-eyed look on your face and the courage to ask for help and have everything you need in under five minutes. They might even set it all up for you. If you're an online shopper, look for a spinning rod and reel combo, a

Small-town East Texas

Fishing is about stillness, listening, looking, and staying present.

net, pliers, line, and hooks. Even better than buying? Borrowing from that friend who's always asking you to go camping.

3. If you're setting up your own gear, lay your rod on a flat surface, grab your line, and open the bail (that's the U-shaped gizmo on your reel). Then feed your line through the closest guide to the reel (those are the little circles on the underside of your rod), tie the line around the spool, and start winding! Don't go too fast, and be sure to leave about one-eighth inch of room from the edge of the spool.

4. When it all looks official, feed about four feet of line through the guides and attach a hook using a sturdy knot. I like a clinch knot. Other than the moment you pull your mighty first catch from the water, this is the one time you can use your phone—and it's only to google "clinch knot."

5. Put your phone away!

6. Find your favorite new fishing spot. My dad likes quiet, brackish-looking spots close to shore with thick underwater vegetation. He hasn't led me astray yet.

7. Bait that hook! This is the messy part. If you're fishing in East Texas, get your hands on some crawfish (live or . . . not live) and poke the hook through the center of his tail, well below the fin so that he doesn't wiggle off or get pinched by a catfish. If you're fishing elsewhere, worms (my go-to) or nightcrawlers work well. If you're squeamish, you can use a lure. Bug guts aren't for everyone.

8. Open the bail, make like Tom Hanks, and cast away! Don't forget to control the line with a gentle hand on the pole so you don't go too far. Close the bail when you're done if it doesn't close automatically.

9. Take a deep breath. Look around. Listen.

10. Repeat as often as possible.

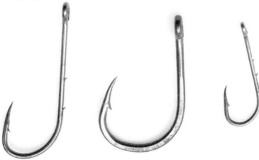

Music *for Driving Across Texas*

If he wanted to, my dad could drive from the Panhandle to Amarillo in complete silence, listening to nothing but the sounds of big-rig horns and tires on the interstate. I love driving with him for the same reasons I love fishing with him. It's a quiet time to think and look and feel. I notice things I normally wouldn't: weird debris by the side of the road, letters that burnt out on restaurant signs and gas stations, and how bright the sun is shining.

Even for stoic creatures like us, though, there comes a time on the road when the weather is right, the sky is cloudless, and everybody can find their sunglasses. Maybe a foot starts tapping or a few lyrics sneak out from our lips. The only thing a person can do under these most perfect conditions is roll down the window, lean back into the seat, and turn on some damn good Texas music. These are some of the Lone Star State's finest road-trippin' jams:

Damn Good Texas Music

"Act Naturally" by Buck Owens • "Castanets" by Alejandro Escovedo •
"Colors" by Black Pumas • "Corpus Christi Bay" by Robert Earl Keen •
"Dearly Departed" by Shakey Graves • "Everyday People" by Sly & The Family Stone
• "Follow Your Arrow" by Kacey Musgraves • "Galveston" by Glen Campbell •
"Hound Dog" by Big Mama Thornton • "I'll Drown in My Tears" by Johnny Winter •
"Is Anybody Goin' to San Antone" by Charley Pride • "I Turn My Camera On" by Spoon
• "La Grange" by ZZ Top • "Lone Star State of Mind" by Nanci Griffith •
"Low Down Rolling Stone" by Gary Clark Jr. • "My Church" by Maren Morris •
"On the Road Again" by Willie Nelson • "Piece of My Heart" by Janis Joplin •
"Single Ladies (Put a Ring on It)" by Beyoncé • "Smooth Sailin'" by Leon Bridges •
"Texas Sun" by Khruangbin & Leon Bridges • "Texas (When I Die)" by Tanya Tucker

Even though the below songs are clearly not Texan,
Dad told me I should add them anyway:

"All Along the Watchtower" by Jimi Hendrix • "In the Garden" by Jim Reeves •
"Moonlight Sonata" by Beethoven • "Oh! Darling" by The Beatles •
Symphony no. 7 in A major, op. 92 by Beethoven •
"Stairway to Heaven" by Led Zeppelin • "The Survivor" by Phil Keaggy

Sundays are for two things: praising Jesus and braising chuck roast.

Mama Pam's *Sunday Pot Roast*

In the Lawless household, Sundays are for two things: praising Jesus and braising chuck roast. You wake up in the morning, get dressed in your hottest modest church clothes (the more gingham, the better), and walk downstairs into a hot, herbaceous steam cloud pouring off the stove. The smell of velvety sage leaves, rendering fat, and a whole head of garlic kissing the stockpot sticks to your hair all day long and reminds you in warm breaths of what's for dinner. By the time church is over, the caramelizing vegetables and grass-fed meat have been roasting for hours and are so potent, they practically meet you halfway home.

Living in the middle of a cattle ranch certainly had its perks, and even though in Nashville we're a little short on space for our own herd, I do my best to re-create the lazy Sunday magic my mom conjures up back home. There's nothing better than ending the week with a full heart and a full belly.

YOU'LL NEED:

1 (3- to 5-pound) chuck or round roast (look for one with lots of marbling!)

2 1/2 teaspoons salt

1 teaspoon garlic powder (or 4 to 5 cloves garlic, chopped) to use as a rub (but use as much garlic as you like—there's never too much)

2 teaspoons black pepper

1 teaspoon dry mustard

2 teaspoons chopped fresh thyme

3 tablespoons canola oil

2 cups red wine or broth

2 bay leaves

1 medium head garlic, peeled and separated into cloves

2 medium white onions, cut into large wedges

4 to 5 fresh sage leaves

2 pounds assorted root vegetables cut into large chunks (I like peeled carrots, parsnips, and potatoes)

1/4 cup Worcestershire sauce

STEPS:

1. Preheat oven to 350 degrees.

2. In a medium bowl, mix salt, garlic powder, pepper, dry mustard, and thyme. Rub all over your roast. Mom also likes to give the roast an extra sprinkling of salt and pepper and a pat of garlic powder (or garlic cloves) at the end.

3. Heat oil over medium-high heat in an oven-safe Dutch oven until shimmering, and sear roast on all sides (about 4 minutes per side). According to Mom, this is the most important step. Lock in those flavors, y'all!

4. Transfer roast to a plate and deglaze the Dutch oven with wine or broth until reduced by half.

5. Return the roast to the Dutch oven and add the bay leaves, garlic cloves, onions, and sage. Cover and cook in the oven for 2 hours, turning roast after 1 hour and unsticking any of those pesky onions. If the roast looks dry, add 1/2 cup broth or water.

6. Remove the Dutch oven from the oven and transfer the meat to a plate, trying oh-so-carefully not to let it fall apart. Add the root-vegetable mix to the Dutch oven and gently place that beautiful-looking roast on top of them. Pour the Worcestershire over the meat, cover, and cook for an additional 45 minutes to 1 hour until the roast's internal temperature reads 145 degrees and the veggies are tender.

7. Place the vegetables and meat on a platter, cover with foil, and let rest for about 10 minutes.

8. If you're a devoted rider of the gravy train like I am, this is a great time to spoon the fat off the cooking liquid, pour the liquid into a medium saucepan, and bring it to a boil on high heat. Let it reduce into a gravy or, if you like it on the thicker side, reduce heat and stir in cornstarch 1 teaspoon at a time until desired consistency is reached. Season with salt and pepper and reserve for serving.

9. Set the table, say your prayers, and get your Sunday supper on!

Homemade

DIY Denim Shorts *(Sorry, Dad!)*

Rebellion looks different on all of us. Some kids stay out past curfew or get secret lower-back tattoos, and other kids grow into adults who'll make a pair of Daisy Dukes (or Daisy Dudes) out of anything denim.

I was raised with a firm Southern Baptist "two inches above the knee" rule when it came to hemlines. My dad would gladly shell out a dollar to any daughter who managed to make it to church in a simple, discreet, God-fearing dress, and at age thirteen I owned more pairs of Bermuda shorts than our local golf pro.

In high school, when I was feeling truly wild, I'd lie on top of the hay bales, roll up the cuffs of my shorts, and let the sun hit my thighs, trying to even out what can only be described as "devout" tan lines. Eventually, after I'd seen enough episodes of *Dawson's Creek* to know better, I marched down to the local Goodwill, bought three battered old pairs of Wrangler jeans, and got out my mom's sewing shears. Even though I rarely made it out of the bedroom in my creations (which was good, because crafting the perfect pair of cutoffs takes years of refining), I sure liked the feeling of cutting loose. Life is too short for long shorts. Let's get snipping!

Life is too short for long shorts.

YOU'LL NEED:

Old denim (Goodwill and Salvation Army are your friends. Or
   your older brother's top dresser drawer . . . sorry, John.)
White or light-colored chalk
Box cutter
Sharp scissors

STEPS:

1. Find a *loose* pair of old denim. Two sizes up is your best bet.
2. Measure 2½ inches on the inseam (or longer if you want) and
   mark with white chalk.
3. Draw a horizontal line across the short (use an old pair for
   reference) and measure the far side of the waistband to the
   line—match this width on both sides and back.
4. Cut along the chalk line on only one side of the fabric at a time.
5. Draw a chalk square where you want to add distressed accents.
6. Using your box cutter, cut slits horizontally ¼ inch apart.
7. Wash, dry, repeat, run them over with your dad's truck /
   brother's four-wheeler, drag them with sandpaper . . . you get it.

CHAPTER 2

Forgotten Dolls

In trying to belong, sometimes we forget that we already do.

My parents' bathroom scale is a thin sheet of glass suspended on small circular risers. They keep it tucked in a corner, and it's the first thing I see when I walk in to shower after running. It has a big blue screen and boxy numbers that shift their shapes while you stand and watch and wait. Compared to the rest of the house, which is warm and well-loved and has the coziness of Christmas all year long, the scale looks like an artifact sent from the future.

I set my foot down and listen to the risers moan as they accept my weight, hating that the little machine announces me that way. My breath gets shallow and my heart shudders as the screen wakes with a flash and begins to flip. I take off my socks, because they might weigh a few ounces, and then my shirt, which is soaking wet from five miles under a big Texas sun and could be good for a half a pound. A charge of adrenaline comes as I watch the numbers, looking down at them as they flicker.

121.4

119.2

120.3

I shift. It helps the numbers settle sometimes.

119.2

I'm exactly where I should be, exactly where I planned to be. My pulse slows, relief comes, and when the screen clicks off and fades to grey, I turn on the shower and stand under a cone of hot water, letting it pour over a body that, today, feels good enough to live in.

Beautiful has changed. It used to be sitting in an aluminum boat and watching the light on the water. It used to be the harmonies of the church choir vibrating through the sanctuary and my mother's smile. Now, it's different. At seventeen, *beautiful* is a thin body covered with lean strips of muscle in precise locations. It's fitting into the smallest size carried at the store and the satisfaction of the right number forming on the blue screen. I'm not sure when it transformed: maybe at twelve, when my body began to take small steps toward womanhood, or at fourteen, when the ladies in town started taking diet pills that made them hyper and drinking pitchers of electric-pink Crystal Light for lunch. They rejoiced with every little bit of themselves that fell away, and I didn't understand. It could have been at sixteen, when I realized that every notable woman on prime-time television, the freeway billboards, and the magazines at the checkout came in only one shape. The message was clear and urgent.

"Don't get fat!"

"Don't be lazy!"

"Count the calories!"

"Join the club!"

"You can do it!"

"WILLPOWER!"

So, like always, I did as I was told. I worked harder. I ran farther. Practiced more. Ate less to become more. I achieved, and now I am what I was told to be. It feels like walking around in armor. The rest of the world can fall apart, my parents can fight, my softball team can lose, my big sisters can move away, as long as I stay perfect in my shell. I am beautiful, and beautiful is safe.

In September of senior year, my skin starts to itch. All I've had to eat in the past twenty-four hours is a navel orange I worried was too big and too sweet to trust myself with. I ate it quickly, swallowing it like a secret and trying to forget I'd ever enjoyed it. Around eleven in the morning, pink, perfectly circular hives rise all at once over my body, and my feet start to swell, pressing against the sides of my shoes. The teacher is talking about tangent formulas, and I'm so dizzy that there are four of her and she sounds like she's speaking underwater. Quietly, I excuse myself to go to the bathroom, but by the time I reach the threshold, I can hardly walk. Everyone is staring.

The faces and colors and world map on the wall swirl together, and I barely make it out of the room before I lose feeling in my legs. I lean against the wall and slide down onto the speckled tile. A friend whose face I struggle to recognize lifts me and, with slow steps, helps me get to the nurse. My skin is grey under the tubes of fluorescent institutional lighting. Something is very wrong, but I'm filled more with shame than worry.

The hours that follow are full of whispers. People talk and my teachers panic. My parents pick me up and take me to the doctor. They're worried, and, though they'd never say it, I'm afraid they're embarrassed. It's a small town; everyone will know, and everyone will secretly, sheepishly love it. The blonde cheerleader, the perfect daughter with perfect grades, will become the perfect cliché. I try to spin it.

It's the heat.

It's the sports.

It's pushing myself too hard.

It's forgetting to eat.

It's everything except the word *anorexia*.

"I've got it. I'll take care of it," I tell my parents that evening when they sit me down in the living room to talk, perched stiffly on a chair that nobody ever sits in.

They nod and don't mention it again. I find a more acceptable weight to sit at, which is still unhealthy but not as alarming. I tell myself I'll get better, and for a day or two, I do. But before long, I eat just four grapes instead of eight; I skip breakfast, then lunch. I binge and purge, and it all comes back.

College comes. I go to the University of Texas at Austin, where everyone is proud to be a Longhorn. I think that being a Longhorn will be much easier than being an eighteen-year-old girl, that magically, on the precipice of adulthood, I'll become sensible and stop worrying about my body, punishing it and controlling it like a bad dog. The pressure intensifies though. Now it's not just about being perfect but perfect *and* grown up. My brain needs calories to eat to get through classes. I feed it, but food feels like a boulder on my belly. I start purging more, hoping it will settle the score between a hungry body and a hungry mind. I do the college things I'm supposed to do: I get a boyfriend who is nice, tall, and also Texan. I play sports, get good grades, work every free moment, love Jesus, maintain a size zero, and plan for the perfect future. I tell myself the world will change—it'll stop telling women to be beautiful while it tells men to be powerful, it'll stop selling us Splenda and them Omaha Steak—but nothing changes. The message stays the same, and so do I.

By fall, I stop noticing when the early sky is illuminated in coral and ballet-slipper pink. I forget the feeling of casting my fishing line into the pond under the shade of the gum tree. Instead, joy is a pair of pants that used to be snug, slipping below my hip bones. I have friends who love me, teachers who believe in me, a boyfriend who is proud to hold my hand, and I manage to have all of it while keeping my secret safe: I'm vibrant on the outside and greying on the inside. I spend all day learning how to nurture sick bodies in nursing school, but I'm living in one. And it gets sicker, weaker, more tired every single day. I'm not hungry anymore, not for anything.

It's nearly Thanksgiving when my cousins catch on. We live together in a small, chic apartment where it's hard to keep secrets. They tell my parents, but I'm so numb I can hardly hear anyone speak.

"I'm so sorry. We had to. We love you," they confess in shaky sobs, dropping me off at home for the holiday break.

Mom and Dad are waiting for me in the living room. It's been freshly vacuumed and polished for the intervention. They tell me they love me, they're worried, and I need to get help. I tell them that everything is under control. As the words leave my mouth, I realize "control" is a big part of the problem. I spend the next few days scared but relieved, ashamed but not alone, and in utter disbelief that I said it out loud and made it real. My parents watch me pick at my food, chasing it around the plate with my spoon. They never noticed the way I eat before because it doesn't look that strange. Suddenly, every meal feels like an audition.

Am I well enough?

Did I eat enough?

Are they still worried?

The day before I drive back to Austin, I make the long walk from the back door to the round bales by the pasture where I used to soak up the sun and dream. I grab the orange twine and pull my body to the top, taking a long sip of the same eighty-degree air I've been breathing since birth. *I'm home.* The black cows are grazing, jaws grinding away and tails flicking. The blond grasses that go on forever sway and shimmer in the low-hanging sun. I hardly see any of it. I'm fixated on my shadow, a collection of dark, vaguely human-shaped sticks. I look more like a sapling than a woman. Staring out at the skies and forever-wide fields used to feel like looking heaven in the eye. Now I can't even bring myself to do it. If I'm home, close to everything and everyone I know, why do I feel like a stranger here?

That night in my childhood bed, covers pulled up to my chin, I feel an ache. *Hunger,* I think at first, and it is, but it's something deeper too. It's yearning and wanting and craving something more. It's looking out at the fifteen dolls still piled in a corner and knowing I haven't had a period in ten months; I might never be a mother. It's homesickness, wanting to feel safe not just in the house I've lived in my whole life but in my own body.

"I need help."

I say it in a whisper, just barely aloud, to the forgotten dolls and God and the dark room. With the last of the words still hanging on my breath, I feel free for the first time in such a long, long time.

When I'm back at school, I find a therapy group. Once a week I sit in a room full of women just like me who have forgotten what *beautiful* really is but desperately want to know it again. I don't speak very much at first, and nobody makes me. I just sit in my white plastic chair, listening to my story told over and over by people I've never met before. Even though I've known all along I wasn't alone in this, it's the first time I've seen it out in the open. The room holds no secrets and allows no shame. It is filled with only brave people. Here, I feel seen, heard, and understood, not as the person I want to be—the one I dress up as and take out into the world—but as the person I really am.

I talk a little in the sessions, but not much. Mostly I think—about the community I've found in the room and the community I've always had outside it but couldn't really see. I think about worried friends, teachers, coaches, and my parents. I think mostly about my parents. I remember the fear in their eyes when they drove me to the doctor at seventeen, still covered in bumps and woozy from nearly losing consciousness at school. I remember the way they watched me eating my mashed potatoes, shifting their eyes whenever I caught them. I think about the unpleasant living room conversations that made my skin itch. All of it was love. In trying to belong, sometimes we forget that we already do.

Hope starts with small things: throwing away the tattered, threadbare journal with the pages covered in numbers and equations and how many calories I ate in a day, and replacing it with a new one I fill with words, little poems, and what I did in a day. I write furiously, as though my little Bic pen marking up the neat cream-colored pages is a matter of life and death. Maybe it is. The most important, wildest, truest words I put down are "I'm not okay. I need help." I write them daily, getting to know them slowly and with care, first telling the truth in a quiet breath before shouting it from a rooftop. I start to talk more in the meetings, and people are kind to me as I stumble over my words and clear my throat too many times. They encourage me and tell me that I'm strong. I start to believe them. None of us are seated in the circle, stepping into recovery in tiny, nervous movements, because we don't belong, but because we do. It's okay to not be okay.

Gently, patiently, and imperfectly, with therapists and books and friends and God, I take a good, long, honest, deep look at who I am. Looking into myself, not *at* myself, I see my true reflection for the first time. I need to control things. I have unacknowledged trauma. I am afraid to disappoint others. I want to be perfect. I want to be loved. I *am* loved. And I am hungry in every way.

The next time I travel back to Marshall and the sun begins to lower its orange shoulders into the earth, I pull my body up easily onto the round bale and watch the sky like it's a movie screen. I feel a sense of home in the rustling grasses, the heat bugs droning low and steady, and in myself. Not knowing whether the feeling will be fleeting or forever, I close my eyes and breathe in deep every smell and sound, committing it to memory with the strength of a promise, the kind of promise a young girl makes to her dolls in play and believes she'll never, ever forget.

Keep SAKES

Forgotten Dolls

There is no place harder or more glorious to live than inside a woman's body. As a child, I was fixated on finding beautiful things in the world; as a teenager, I was determined to become one. I didn't know who I was, and I didn't know where to look. To someone who was lost in the confusion of high school, hormones, and a home life where we didn't exactly sit down for fireside chats about our deep, aching feelings, the clarity was a relief. Conformity and control felt safer than creativity. I became who I believed I was supposed to be, but I ended up losing who I was in the process.

I have been healing from disordered eating for nearly two decades now. Decades that have been filled with individual therapy, journaling, self-love, honesty, and knowing when to ask for help. Though I'm in recovery, I don't consider myself recovered. I love my body, I honor it, and I trust it, but it is still a challenge to enjoy food some days. I still struggle with accountability. I'm still learning how to talk about it all and to reconcile my role in the fashion and social media spaces, knowing the images and ideas they project can reinforce unrealistic, unhealthy ideals. The one thing I don't want to do is not talk about it. It's okay to not be okay. Healing looks different on all of us, but it always looks good.

It's okay to not be okay.

Blank Page

In the tender, clumsy days of early recovery, I went to the UT bookstore and bought a new journal. It was orange, cheap, and ugly, but it became the safest space on earth to me. Those flimsy spiral-bound papers taught me how to feel again—or, rather, revealed to me what I always had been feeling but never knew how to express.

I was bad at first. Conversing with myself felt more like meeting a shifty Tinder date than an old friend, and even in the loving space of a blank page, I struggled to be honest with myself. Journaling isn't storytelling; it's truth-telling, and nothing is as uncomfortable, intimate, or illuminating as the bare-assed, pock-marked, dimply, fully naked truth. Even though it hurt sometimes, as promised, it also set me free. It was worth every sweaty, stressed-out moment of reflection.

These days I get plenty of writing in for work, but still, nothing is as challenging *or* as healing to me as journaling. When I get stuck (which I totally do), these prompts never fail to get the pen rolling.

1. When was the last time you trusted yourself?
2. What made you laugh today?
3. Whom do you miss?
4. Where do you feel the most at peace?
5. What do you need to feel safe today?
6. When do you feel the most beautiful?
7. Whom can you forgive?
8. Why are you proud of yourself?

The greatest gift I have ever given myself is the truth.

Work in Progress

I'm not sure a person can be bad at talk therapy, but I cut it real close.

As I did with everything else in life, I started my healing journey as if it were a hundred-meter dash. I wanted to win! Succeed! Break every record for self-improvement that had ever been set! (Thankfully, there are none.) By my third session, at peak keenness, I asked the therapist how I was doing.

She looked at me puzzled, like, *You tell me. Isn't that why we're here?*

Therapy changed my life, but at times, it was a rocky road for this weary traveler. It took me two years to stop trying to "win" at recovery. I've had to get to know and accept myself, learn to identify triggers, and then practice how to respond to them. I've had to forgive myself, which, honestly, wasn't the psychological Parisienne picnic I hoped it would be. If you're just getting started, go easy on yourself, have grace for yourself, and don't give up on yourself. Here are a few little lessons about getting help that I learned along the way.

LOOK AT YOURSELF AS A WHOLE PERSON

We're so much more than our legs or stomachs or mistakes or bad habits. I find it really easy to fixate on what feels wrong and forget what is right. I keep a picture of myself at four years old taped to the bathroom mirror. When I feel like I'm going nowhere, it reminds me how far I've come.

RECOVERY IS NOT LINEAR

Healing takes time, and there is nothing quick or perfect about it. For plenty of us, it is a lifelong journey that takes patience, determination, and unending amounts of compassion for ourselves. You might take one step forward and three steps backward. I know I did.

YOU DON'T NEED TO DO IT ALL BY YOURSELF

Even though I love to do things with my own two hands, the support, love, community, and accountability (as scary as it may sound) of others has been key for me. Even letting in just one person can make a big difference.

DON'T BUY ALL THE SELF-HELP BOOKS

In my first year of treatment, I think I bought about fifty titles. I was drowning in advice—some of it great, some of it not so great, lots of it conflicting. Wait for something that connects. Don't overwhelm yourself. Take it one page at a time.

GET HONEST AND STAY HONEST

The greatest gift I have ever given myself is the truth; it's where I've found freedom, forgiveness, self-acceptance, and deep love. There are a lot of things in this world worth hiding from, but your most authentic self is not one of them.

DON'T GIVE UP!

Chances are, there will be a session where you go through the whole cube of Kleenex and never want to go back. You will be puffy and red, and someone in the Walgreens will ask if you had a chemical peel. (This will make you cry harder.) Keep showing up. Keep digging deep. Keep learning. I'm sure glad I did.

Antoinette at Her Dressing Table, Mary Cassatt, 1909

Beauty School

Feeding my body differently meant feeding my mind differently too. Through my formative years, I probably consumed a few too many images of beauty queens and Barbie dolls. It's no wonder that the ideas I developed around physical appearance, fitness, femininity, and sexuality were unhealthy, insular, and wildly unrealistic. I needed to open my eyes wider, just like I'd done as a child.

I looked at artwork, went people watching, read stories, explored new places, and listened to new music, and at every single turn, I found exquisite, unforgettable, admirable women. None of them were supermodels; all of them were breathtaking. Reframing beauty made beauty easier to find, even in myself. I'm still working at it, but it's good work.

If you're scrolling, stop. If you're crash dieting, don't. If you don't think you look right, look again. One kind of beautiful is a hundred kinds of wrong.

Seated Bather, Pierre-Auguste Renoir, 1883

Portrait of Jean Samary,
Pierre-Auguste Renoir,
1877

Spanish Girl Leaning on a Window Sill,
Mary Cassatt, 1872

One kind of beautiful is a hundred kinds of wrong.

Mujer indígena con cempasúchil (*Indian Woman with Marigold*),
Felipe Gutiérrez, 1876

CHAPTER 3

Wedding Ring

If it isn't the true thing, it can't be the right one.

I drive to Crossroads Baptist Church in a silver Camry with my bushy white dress in a garment bag. I'm getting married today, June 20, a day we picked because it worked for our parents and it would give us enough time to go on a beach vacation before school started back up again.

I'm nervous. My stomach has been sick for weeks.

He's a good man.

We'll have a good life.

Grow up. It's time to grow up. You're not a kid anymore.

I tell myself these things over and over. I'm doing the right thing, whether it feels that way or not. I park the car under a redbud and breathe deep.

The church is almost empty when I walk inside, hauling my enormous dress in its black vinyl cocoon. Women from the florist shop arrange bunches of white roses in the sanctuary, singing to themselves like Snow White's cheerful militia of birds and draping long swaths of organza down the sides of the aisle. I've walked the distance from the door to the pulpit a thousand times, to take communion, carol with the children's choir at Christmas, and sometimes just to stare up at the two-story-tall crucifix and wonder if maybe something a little smaller would have been plenty glorious and fit better in the space.

I smile at the ladies as they work, fluffing the baby's breath like it's Texas hair and sniffing at the tea roses, getting high on their own supply. They wave at me and shout hello, voices echoing across a room that for years was floor-to-ceiling carpet but now feels a bit like a concert venue. Pastor Rice's car pulls up into its spot and he gives me a gentle nod through the front window. He's got his fancy Roman collar on. It's a big day for everyone. I've been a part of his family here practically since I've been a part of my own.

He's a good man, I remind myself again.

The lights in the Sunday school classroom are off when I walk inside, and everything smells the way it always has, like the thin pages of children's hymnals and white glue. I prod the light switch, which is stiff and ungiving. With a *snap*, the flat plastic panels glow to life and I look around, reliving the years I spent here with the kids from town making bedazzled Popsicle-stick crucifixes and paper snowflakes, sitting quietly, crisscross-applesauce, while our teacher, sweet Mrs. Betty Raley, casually read to us about the beheading of John the Baptist. I hang my dress in the back closet next to a giant ball of tinsel and plastic bins of Christmas decorations. The dress is so big that even sheathed in the garment bag, the door won't shut all the way.

When the stylist arrives fifteen minutes later to do my hair, I've been rocking in the chair they use to soothe the fussy babies. She scuttles around in a cloud of Dillard's perfume getting her supplies together, face scarlet from the heat. There's the Aqua Net and the bobby pins. The big round brush and the Goody mirror. She also has a shopping bag full of curlers resting in the crook of her elbow in case of emergency. The only way to fix bad hair in Texas is to turn it into big hair.

"Can you believe it, Mary?!" she says softly, shaking her head. "You're getting married."

I *can* believe it. Everybody here gets married by twenty-two. You get married by twenty-two. You have one baby by twenty-three and three by thirty. *He*, whoever he might be, goes to work and you stay home in a euphoria of wobbly first steps, slow-cooker meals, and yoga DVDs. You might have a career as something virtuous, a teacher or—like me—a nurse, but inevitably you'll be most celebrated for your noble and tireless service to the family at home. Somewhere in the middle, you become more of a woman than a girl. Maybe it's when you pay a mortgage or give your heart away. Maybe it happens when you lose your virginity or cook your first Thanksgiving meal. He becomes a man, too, or at least it gets easier for him to grow a beard.

The stylist ushers me over to a preschool chair next to the full-length mirror that somebody, maybe Mrs. Raley, brought in so that I could behold myself in white before my husband does.

I'm doing the right thing. He's the right one. This is how it's supposed to be. My stomach murmurs a warning that I ignore.

She gathers my hair and twists it into an easy updo she's made ten thousand times before. She does all the ladies' church hair and has for years.

"Hold your breath now," she instructs me.

I seal my lips, shut my eyes, and disappear behind a veil of Aqua Net. When she's done, she grabs her pink paddle-shaped mirror and shows me the back. Her mouth is small and tense, making no secret of the fact that she would have preferred more Dallas, less New York. I love it though. I look like a bride, a woman, someone who is certain.

"You remind me so much of Sam," she sings sweetly to my reflection, smiling at my dad's nose and perpetually furrowed brow.

I do look like my dad, but today I see his mother, Alta-Mae, too.

Because God is good and genetics are real, I ended up with my grandma's body: a long, angular, and graceful vessel that probably should have gone to a dancer. Alta-Mae never danced. She dressed—in sophisticated monochromatic suits; modern, architectural hats; and the most perfect, balanced accessories. She put on Paris to go to the Piggly Wiggly and didn't care what anybody said.

Perched on her lap at five years old, I would meditate on how beautiful she was, how confident and creative, how different—and *different* is not something people here make a habit of being. I'd sit with her as long as she'd let me, just taking her in, examining the delicate links on her buttery gold necklaces and losing myself in the cushion-cut diamond Grandpa put on her finger when he got back from the war. He adored her, even though she dressed more like Grace Kelly than a rancher's wife, even though she spent as much time painting her nails as she did cooking dinner. Now they rest together under a pink granite headstone across town.

That'll be us one day, I think, picturing the man who will be my husband, who is kind and handsome and appropriate in every way, but can't know me well enough to love me. I don't even know myself.

The thought knocks the wind from me and I swallow slowly.

You can do this! my brain assures me.

But should you? my heart asks again.

Giving my shoulder one last squeeze, my stylist leaves me to go Aqua Net her own hair. I stay busy rearranging the plastic nativity set on the bookshelf. Jesus is the size of a bean, Mary looks like Joni Mitchell, and the donkey is missing an ear.

I begin to hear more people outside my little room as it gets closer to the time stamped on the invitation. The organist is practicing his Wagner, and I take it as my cue to get ready. I'm going for the "pure" look and I don't need to try very hard. I wear only enough makeup to make sure my face doesn't totally disappear in the photos, filling my brows in lightly and landing somewhere between Ernie, who has no eyebrows, and Bert, who really only needs the one. My lips are stained cranberry and I don't bother with cheeks because the thermostat in the corner says eighty-one. I'm blushing enough for seventeen brides.

Slowly, step-by-step, practicing for the aisle, I walk to the closet, remove the weighty black bag, and lay it on a table, which still has a few shiny spots from the Sunday school's manic use of glitter glue. The zipper moans as I pull it down, and the enormous hundred-layer dress gives a rustling sigh, happy to be sprung from jail. I step into it and pull the stiff bodice up to my chest. I'm equal parts pastry and princess.

There's a soft knock at the door, and my mom comes to help me do up the never-ending procession of white buttons that march from my tailbone to the middle of my back. She stands facing me and squeezes my hands, which are clammy and pale. Growing up, after I lost a softball game or scored *second* best on a quiz, being near my mom was the only comfort in the world. She didn't need to say anything; she just needed to be with me. I want to feel better today, but even with her hands on mine, I can't.

Her eyes water. She couldn't have designed a better husband for her daughter. She couldn't have prayed a brighter future into existence. She's so, so proud. My sisters come next in an orange satin blur. Neither looks particularly thrilled with their bridesmaid's dress. Neither looks particularly thrilled that I'm getting married, though they both do their best to hide it. They've each taken me aside a few times over the past several months to ask if maybe I'm a bit too young. Today they keep their worries to themselves, tucked behind a wall of tangerine fabric.

I wait for someone to ask me if I'm sure, *really* sure, but nobody does. Mom tells me I look beautiful and I thank her profusely. She says she can't believe it. I say I can't either. She hugs me, tighter and longer than she ever has before. We follow the wedding-day script that mothers and daughters have been using in the South forever and ever.

"I love y'all," I tell them, eyes filling halfway, panic setting in.

"We love you too." My mom smiles. They go off to join the bridal party.

Dad comes to get me just two minutes before the ceremony is set to begin. I can hear my friend Lisa singing the first notes of "Amazing Grace" as I leave the schoolroom with my arm curled around his. Slowly, slowly, slowly the mothers begin taking their seats near the front of the room and people hush their children.

"I'm proud of you," he says, which might be my favorite thing he (or anyone) ever says to me: the perpetual achiever, the kid who snuck out of bed at 1 a.m. to practice her jump shot, the student who was never the smartest but worked the hardest and just wanted to make everyone happy.

Just shy of the aisle we stop, and he hands me a sap-green jewelry box. I'd recognize it anywhere. The velour is balding over the soft corners just like I remember, and it smells, just a bit, like her closet. I crack the lid and my grandmother's cushion-cut diamond is waiting for me, set sturdy on a pair of gem-spangled gold bands brilliant enough to compete with the brazen center stone I've loved my entire life.

"She would have wanted you to have it today," he says softly, and I believe him. She would have wanted me to have everything I wanted.

The old Canon in D starts to play, and I wish for a second that it didn't feel quite so much like the wedding "march" that it is. I slip my arm back through my father's and slide Alta-Mae's diamond onto my right ring finger. Looking down at it, more beautiful than the big dress and the big day, I begin to cry. A quiet string of tears rolls down my cheeks because it means more to have her ring than it will to wear the one that the man at the altar has waiting in his pocket.

The gold band warms to my skin.

Oh boy.

I trust God and my mom, the way things are and always have been. I wish I could trust myself that way.

I walk down the aisle at a perfectly measured pace toward a perfectly measured life, trembling as much as the boning of my dress will let me. I see him waiting in his tuxedo and the pink drains from my cheeks. I go from somebody's daughter to somebody's wife in a little under an hour, passing over the part where I become Mary altogether. We are jubilant and grinning, more relieved that it's over than excited to begin a life together. We kiss and hold each other's faces in our hands. They weep and throw rice. The limo rolls clumsily around the corner. Everything is right.

But if it isn't the true thing, it can't be the right one.

Keep SAKES

Wedding Ring

At twenty-two, I only knew what love was on paper. It was a big wedding with big hair, my first sips of Prosecco, a good man. I had endless faith in my family, my friends, my church, but hardly any in myself. Learning to listen to my intuition, summoning the courage to call it a gut feeling instead of indigestion, has taken time. Following those feelings, trusting mystery over certainty, has taken even longer.

In a little church schoolroom cooled to eighty-one degrees, lost in a big white wedding dress, with 350 people waiting in the pews, 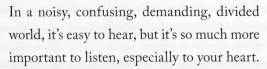I heard my heart speak for the first time. Though that day I may have hushed it and carried on, it didn't keep quiet for long.

In a noisy, confusing, demanding, divided world, it's easy to hear, but it's so much more important to listen, especially to your heart.

At twenty-two,
I only knew what love
was...

Red Flags

My gut is great at waving the red flag, but my brain isn't always so good at waving the white one. Most days my intellect wrestles any little inklings into submission before they stand a chance at taking root. As much as I wish it weren't true, I really have to work to stay connected, and though I don't always know what it looks like when I *am* in tune, I do know what it looks like when I'm not.

SCREEN TIME IS UP

This is less my heart and more "the weekly update from my phone," but if I'm too absorbed in the relentless Instaworld, there's a good chance I'm not very present in the actual world. It isn't just the time on the screen either; it's the time I spend stressing about it. I'm straight up missing the big picture if I'm outside on a pretty day wondering, *Was it the right tone? The right number of words? The right picture?*

SLEEP IS DOWN

In paradise, we would all sleep for nine hours and wake up with the sun for muesli, push-ups, and an hour of personal reflection. No matter how clued in to myself I get, this will never happen. *But* if I'm struggling to fall asleep, waking up exhausted, or having wacky dreams at night, quite often there's something I'm avoiding during the day.

I FEEL SICK

Maybe it was the burrito bowl or maybe I shouldn't take on that new client. Either way, when my body is barking at me, it's time to stop, rest, run, breathe, and think.

I'M JUMPY

If I've had less than three cups of coffee and I scream when the toast pops up, it's safe to say my body has switched to flight mode. I can carry fear around for a long time without acknowledging or isolating it, and I'm fairly certain it isn't peanut butter on seven-grain. When I get keyed up, I cue the deep breathing and personal-inventory taking.

THE PAGE IS BLANK

Creator's block happens to all of us from time to time, but for me, sometimes there's a more significant barrier. I can have plenty to say but suddenly lose the language to say it. In these moments, instead of pushing through, I'm trying to pull back. *Is there something else I should be doing with the time? Am I not in love with the project? Do I need a break?*

Do I need a break?

Texas Hair

Texas girls stick to their roots, except when it comes to coiffing. Under the heat of Friday night lights and our fathers' watchful eyes, we kept our hemlines long but hiked our hair way up to heaven. Coming of age in a conservative community where there wasn't oodles of room for self-expression, hair was one place I could go big—real big—without fear of moral reproach. And you better believe that I did. I made the best of life in a spray-it, don't-say-it culture and fast became an expert at fluffy, flammable, totally fabulous Texas hair.

YOU'LL NEED:

A blow-dryer
6 to 8 self-grip curlers
2- to 3-inch round brush
Hairspray!

STEPS:

1. **WASH IT.** Texture is the enemy of Texas hair. While day-to-day I love a greasy, grungy, lived-in look, any extra weight is going to sink your hairdo like sin on a Sunday (remember, this is Bible country). You can use your regular product, but go easy on any leave-in treatments; we're in a "no pomade" zone.

2. **DRY IT.** Air- or blow-dry (using your fingers) until hair is damp and spray all over with volumizing product. Using a 2- to 3-inch round brush, pulling up and away from the face, dry hair in sections. Look! You're closer to God already!

3. **CURL IT.** My brave Texan ancestors would use anything from soda cans to tube socks as curlers, but I prefer the real deal. Set self-grip curlers (so much easier!) and spray. I just do the crown of my head, but if you're feeling fancy, you can go all the way.

4. **SPRAY IT.** This step is known as the "big spray." When my hair is setting, I close my eyes, hold my breath, say a little prayer, and give it all a good misting.

5. **FREE IT.** When your hair is cool and ready for liftoff (20 to 25 minutes for me, but it may be different for you), liberate those locks and shake it out!

6. **FLIP IT.** This is the fun part. Turn your head over and give it a flip. Because we want more Dolly Parton, less Dee Snider, spray it just one more time.

7. If all else fails, **BUMP IT.** I'm not saying I have used one of these magical, underrated contraptions when pressed for time. But I'm also not saying I haven't. Don't knock it till you've bumped it.

Off Cuts

Alta-Mae Lawless was my first fashion icon and also the world's coolest grandma. Her style was effortless and effervescent. She knew how to use color and shape. She made crazy-good angel food cake with fresh strawberries and could pick a statement piece like nobody else. I loved everything she wore, but of all the mules, minks, and mohair sweaters, nothing took my breath away like that cushion-cut diamond on her finger. Because of that ring, that unexpected, one-of-a-kind, ridiculously sparkly sparkler, I'll never pass up an estate sale or make it out of one without something shiny.

If you're ready to put a ring on it, take a peek at your local antique market, vintage store, or auction house before hitting the big-name bauble broker and keep your eyes peeled for my favorite cuts.

Alta-Mae Lawless

Rose Cut

Similar at first glance to the super-popular brilliant cut, the rose cut covers the same surface area, but often for a fraction of the cost. Since it's normally flat on the bottom, it appears larger in weight than it actually is. The low profile makes the rose cut easy to wear, and what it may not bring in brilliance, it more than makes up for in old-world charm.

Cushion Cut

I just can't get enough of these pillow-shaped pretties! The cushion cut is timeless, romantic, and a wonderful choice if you're looking for an engagement ring that's plenty fun to peek at but doesn't scream "We're getting married!" every time it catches the sun.

Emerald Cut

I never wanted to love the emerald cut, but I do. The first time I put one on, it felt gaudy, like I had a full-length mirror on my hand. Ten minutes in, I'd been transported so deep into a 1930s Miami Beach Deco dreamscape that I could hardly find my way out. There's just something so glamorous about those straight, symmetrical facets and big flashes of light.

Marquise Cut

A jeweler once told me that in the eighteenth century, King Louis XV commissioned the marquise cut to look like the lips of his lover, and I've swooned over it ever since. Long, luxurious, and very sexy, the marquise cut gets me weak in the knees every time.

CHAPTER 4

Breakfast Margaritas

In our strange little world, where life is delicate and one breath makes no promise to the next, love keeps us strong. Coming together is what keeps us from falling apart.

It's 7:06 a.m. and Linda's talking about a tricky vascular patient in need of a valve replacement. I can hear her all the way out on the sidewalk before I've even begun to throw my shoulder into the door. Her voice is big but tired, cutting in and out like a bad radio station, spent from last night's shift and the years of night shifts that came before it. There are five nurses huddled around a small table, all in blue, all laughing, held tenderly in the neon aura of the Corona sign. Otherwise, the bar is empty, as it should be when the sun is still rising.

I plop myself between Maria from San Antonio and Jodie, a bottle blonde and mom of three grown kids. She's been in nursing nearly as long as Linda has, but is less of a cowboy about it.

"Here you go, sweetie," she smiles, squeezing my hand and grabbing me a menu from the stack next to the Cholula. Not that I need it; we've been coming to Bodega's three mornings a week for the past six months. It's just a few blocks from Memorial Hermann, and at the end of our twelve-hour shifts where we care for the human heart in so, so many ways, this is where we come to care for our own. While most of Houston sleeps, we keep watch, monitoring vitals and endless beeps and alarms, managing drips and lines, holding hands, and constantly

59

reassessing. As our own families wake, wipe the sleep from their lashes, check the traffic on I-45, and wait on the coffee to finish brewing, we take the edge off. Or at least, we try.

I wanted to be a nurse early on, almost immediately after I gave up the fantasy of professional bass fishing. Nursing felt like an honorable thing to do, something that would make my parents proud and my husband proud and God proud. I wanted to be a helper. Little did I know it would change my life forever. From a distance the work seemed simple: care for people, serve them, sit with them. But nothing is simple about the space we occupy, the tender gap between life and death where miracle and tragedy chase each other like dogs down the hall.

I started my career in the neonatal ICU, which was a mistake. I thought I'd be a perfect fit because I love babies; instead, I was a terrible fit because I love babies. I walked into the NICU on my first day and walked right back out again. Small bodies bending and bowing while the machines do their breathing, mothers' breasts leaking milk for the children they were meant to feed but never will—it was all too much. I couldn't help anyone. I could hardly even move. I transferred to the cardiovascular ICU where 95 percent of my patients are adults and 60 percent of them laugh at my jokes.

A new waiter, who is skinny and looks about fifteen, drops a pitcher of green margaritas at our table. He's got just a feather of a mustache and no body fat at all. Obviously he has been told to expect us. He doesn't startle when Linda gets loud, Maria cusses in Spanish, or somebody wants an extra shot. He flips on the big TV next to the bar before we can even ask, knowing that we like to watch the weatherman shuffle and point at sunshines and wiggly bacon-shaped heat lines. We will miss the day he's mapping out for us, but we like to watch anyway.

Anna walks up to our table looking like hell, spit straight out of a Gulf storm. Her hair is matted, and two Bic pens stick out of her carrot-colored bun. If she's anything like me, she's probably forgotten that she put them there. Quietly, she pulls up a seat and watches the meteorologist draw his clumsy blue lines on the map. Anna and I hardly know each other—she's been with us only a month.

Her eyes dart suddenly to my hands. I've been tearing little bits from my paper napkin and rolling them between my fingers. When I try to stop, my fingers shake.

"You okay?" she asks.

I nod, clinking my glass against hers and retreating into the wonderfully easy decisions of the laminated menu I don't need: Two tacos or three? Potatoes or refried beans? Chorizo or chicken tinga?

She doesn't take her giant green eyes off me. I take a long, shocking sip of mostly tequila and begin to flutter down from the last few hours.

I lost Charles around midnight. He'd gotten a valve replaced and went into cardiac arrest out of nowhere, just hours after the procedure. His family had been allowed to see him once in recovery while he was sedated and peaceful with a half smile on his face. They'd delighted in the rising and falling of his belly, the color in his cheeks, how strong he looked. I liked them right away, but I like all my families. The kids called him "Daddy" even though they were all grown and greying. They joined hands and prayed over him in one swift motion, like it was something they'd done together hundreds of times before. They talked about a house at the lake they'd take him to when he was all better.

His wife asked me about the IV pole and the numbers on the screen. She wanted to know if it was okay to touch his hand and his hair. Nobody knows the rules when a person they love is asleep, not quite a part of our world or the next one.

"Yes, you can touch his hand."

"Yes, this is his breathing tube."

"Of course, we can get him another blanket."

"No, that beep is nothing to worry about."

"His body temperature is 98.6."

"His blood pressure looks good."

We can provide no certainty about the future, so we tell them what the never-ending collection of lines and drips do, what time the doctor was last in, how much medicine he's on and what it does. We can say only what is true in the moment.

"Thank you for everything, Mary," she smiled, looking down at her husband and breathing a long sigh that sounded something like relief. "I guess we'll go on to the hotel and get some rest then."

"I'll take care of him as if he is my own. I promise you that." I smiled back, watching them file out the door and toward the elevator bank.

Less than thirty minutes later, he was gone. I never took my eyes off of him. His heart was beating, every number looked normal, he presented okay, and then it stopped. We tried to save him—six nurses, two doctors, a respiratory therapist—but we couldn't.

"Mary, you sure you're okay?" Anna asks again, graciously stopping me from playing it all on a loop in my head.

"I think so. I will be."

I lick the salt from the edge of my glass and feel my eyes begin to fill. Anna grabs my hand. For the first time, I grab back.

I look around the table at the women I work with. Besides our work, we have very little in common. Some of us are ending our careers and some are beginning. Some of us believe in God and some don't. We're not all friends, but we're all connected. We've mourned together and celebrated, said things that we don't mean and things that mean absolutely everything. We've bitten our nails to the quick waiting on Life Flight patients and made giant togas from the big, blue isolation sheets, laughing until we ached. We've leaned on one another, and learning to lean has been as crucial an education as microbiology and clinical theory. In our strange little world, where life is delicate and one breath makes no promise to the next, love keeps us strong. Coming together is what keeps us from falling apart.

Our tacos arrive just a few minutes later, at seven forty-five, in a village of steaming baskets that drip with translucent orange pork fat and the stink of raw white onion.

"Eat something." Anna smiles. "You'll feel better."

The seven of us eat quietly but mightily, leaving nothing for the big black rats who visit the dumpster out back. Grease trickles from my chin onto my sleeve and I'm almost too tired to notice it. I dab indifferently at the stain and wish for the energy to stay up a little longer. Out the window, the sun is getting higher in the sky—we'll all go home to sleep soon.

"Better chorizo than diarrhea, right?" Maria grins, nodding toward the fluorescent orange splotch on my scrubs and handing me another napkin.

"At least diarrhea comes out in the wash," I shrug, mouth half full.

She howls for a full minute. Not many people think I'm funny, but Maria is sure that I'm Steve Martin in drag.

A kitchen worker comes in and another after that. It's close to 9 a.m. now. The pitcher is near empty, and our little baskets of food are mostly just onion, shriveled lime skins, and assorted rubble. The cooks punch their cards and give us long, puzzled looks. Linda pours the last of the drink into my glass and winks at me. Our work could easily be lonely, but we don't let it drift that way. Instead, when we clock out, backs aching, feet swollen in our big rubber shoes, we sit down for a meal like the family that we are.

The street swells with traffic noise, and a man in a good suit with a coffee mug arrives to place a catering order. That's our cue. Last call for vampires. Gathering our purses, stretching our spines, and tossing a few extra bucks in for the waiter, we say goodbye and head back to our people. Our *other* people.

"So you're okay?" Anna prods once more before we go, backpack slung on her shoulder.

"Yeah." I smile. "I just needed something to eat."

But what I really needed was Maria's laugh and tequila and a full table and Anna's hand. What I needed was the tacos with the green sauce and the stories Linda likes to tell about her daughter's boyfriend's dog. I needed to be reminded that I'm not doing this alone, and I'm not supposed to. When my family doesn't understand, this one does. When my friends don't know what to say, these ones do. In this work, we take care of one another.

Shaking off the darkness of the bar and the hospital and the long night, I walk out into the sun-filled bustle the weatherman promised us, knowing that it could change at any moment. If it does, there's nothing wrong with taking shelter.

Nurses and hospital workers, if you're reading this, thank you for . . .

the long hours.

the right words.

the extra steps.

the patience. The unending, otherworldly patience.

the compassion.

seeing us.

laughing with us.

crying with us.

never judging.

always caring.

xo

Keep SAKES

Breakfast Margaritas

I was raised in Marshall, Texas, but I grew up in Memorial Hermann. I worked four years at Houston's Texas Medical Center and two more at Vanderbilt in Nashville, and I learned more in those badly lit hallways and tiny rooms than I've learned anywhere else. I learned that life is beautiful, but that death can be beautiful too. I learned that I could laugh and cry in the same thirty minutes, with equal conviction. I learned about hearts, mine most of all.

A nurse sits in the grey area between life and death, and she learns as much about the human spirit as the human body. Every day she witnesses resilience, humility, bravery, and love, all more staggeringly and impossibly deep than most can imagine. Walking through cool hallways and drinking in sour hospital air, I developed true grit and true gratitude. I learned what it was to be strong for someone, and also what it meant to need strength, to lean on others, and to let them lift me.

Another day, another word, another opportunity is never guaranteed to any of us, but while we are here, we're here together, and I believe we're at our best that way.

The World *According to Nurses*

Nursing is a physical and spiritual grind, but the people I worked with and the patients I treated taught me more about tenderness, humanity, and connectedness than a single person deserves to know in her lifetime. I may not remember every name or face or ailment, but I remember the lessons, the depth of people's hearts, the beauty of their minds, the way they held one another and spoke to me. If you're short on wisdom, truth, or strength, sit down with a nurse and ask them to tell you a story. I promise they'll say something that sticks with you. If you don't believe me, check out just a few gems that history's great nurses have left us with.

"I will not allow my life's light to be determined by the darkness around me."

—Sojourner Truth

"Very little can be done under the spirit of fear."

—Florence Nightingale

"Work more and better the coming year than the previous year."

—Mary Eliza Mahoney

"Every evil has its good, and every ill an antidote."

—Dorothea Dix

"Unless I am allowed to tell the story of my life in my own way, I cannot tell it at all."

—Mary Seacole

Time is a great restorer, and changes surely the greatest sorrow into a pleasing memory.

—Mary Seacole

"Patriotism is not enough. I must have no hatred or bitterness towards anyone."

—Edith Cavell

"I have a commission from the Lord God Almighty to do all I can for every miserable creature who comes in my way. He's always sure of two friends—God and me!"

—Mother Bickerdyke

Anatomy of a Good Margarita

Truthfully, tequila and I are no longer in a relationship, and all it took to tear us apart forever was one too-small dinner and a twenty-first birthday party. (Sorry about your car, Brad and LB!) We did have a good run though, and thankfully, I look back on those post-shift margarita breakfasts with my team with nothing but love. And though I may not be any good at *drinking* margaritas, I'm damn good at making them. There's nothing I'd rather do at the end of a long day (or night) than hook someone up with a stiff drink. Here's a look inside the perfect margarita.

Hook someone up with a stiff drink.

START HERE *(if you're feeling fancy)*

1. Pour kosher salt and ancho chili powder (optional) onto a small plate and make a small incision (hospital speak) in a lime wedge.
2. Place the wedge on the edge of the glass and run it all the way around before setting aside.
3. Overturn the glass on the plate, shifting it until the salt sticks. Shake off any extra.

START HERE *(if you're feeling like you want that margarita yesterday)*

1. Fill a shaker with ice and add 2 ounces of *high-quality* tequila blanco. Trust me, if you want to preserve your relationship with margaritas, go top shelf.
2. Add 1 ounce triple sec and the juice of one lime (roughly 1/2 ounce).
3. Shake for 10 to 15 seconds and strain into a highball (or a rocks glass or a coffee mug . . .).
4. Garnish with a wedge of lime and an orange wheel. If you like a little extra sweetness (I do!), add a squeeze of fresh orange instead of simple syrup.
5. Enjoy! (*But not too much!*)

Truest *and Bluest*

In critical care, we could wear one thing, in one color, day in, day out, every last one of us: blue scrubs.

For my personal style journey, these restrictions were not great. I was young, ready to express myself, and *real* hot and bothered about fashion. All I wanted to do was experiment with clothing, but all I *could* do was dress like the genie from *Aladdin* (and he wore it best). It was not ideal, but now I'm a de facto expert in blue scrubs. I can detect the nuances between a turquoise and a Tiffany, a cornflower and a periwinkle, and I can pair anything from a throw pillow to a pair of pants with the exact perfect shade.

At first it all felt a bit limiting, but before long I was putting together sketches for a line of scrubs and stealing Sherwin-Williams paint samples for inspiration. I learned to take great pride in being on the blue team. And I'm still proud.

If you're not gaga for Gonzo, don't despair. I assure you, there's a blue for everything and everyone and with the right silhouette, scrubs can be sexy!

I can detect the nuances between a turquoise and a Tiffany.

CHAPTER 5

Living Room

I loved the plan . . . until I met the dream.

The mouth of the U-Haul opens wide and releases a gust of breath that smells like wet cardboard and moving blankets. A flossy string hangs down from the steel of its upper lip, and there's a giant graphic of a horseshoe crab emblazoned on its side. The truck is from Delaware, which, according to a series of fact-filled decals, is the buckle of the horseshoe-crab belt.

The backs of my knees are sweating. Nashville in July isn't as hot as summertime in Texas, but the air here is thicker and sweeter. It's like sucking honey into your lungs. Everything moves slowly—the young, rubbery leaves on the magnolia tree in front of the house, the neighbor's fat flan-colored cat, me. I'm leaving today, saying goodbye to the home my husband and I have lived in and tried in for the past twelve months, to the marriage we've lived in and tried in for the past five years.

"Do you want us to come with you?" the boys ask, one tall and skinny and one tall and very skinny, both full of Red Bull.

They go to the high school down the road. One of them is my best friend's stepson, and the other, though you'd never know it, plays linebacker on the football team. I hired them to help me, though I think they would have done it for free. They're probably not that much stronger than I am, but they're keen, excited about driving the truck, excited to make easy money, excited to go to Chipotle later and spend all the money on burrito bowls.

I think about it a minute. I would like nothing less than for them to come with me.

"I'm all good. Just give me five minutes, then come on in, okay?"

They're so engrossed in horseshoe-crab facts, I'm not even sure they hear me.

I step onto the stoop and slide the key off its ring, knowing it will stay behind under the brown pot or in the mailbox, knowing that this is the last time I'll unlock the tacky old door. I slide the key into the hole for the last time and it sticks. Everything in this weather is bloated—the dead bolt, the hydrangeas in the garden, my ankles. Finally, I jiggle it the right way, the door opens, and the air conditioner pulls me inside.

The lights are off, which is no surprise. He's a surgeon and every detail of every day is important, especially light switches. Mercifully, he's forgotten the ceiling fan, which is old and looks like it belongs over the salad bar at Ruby Tuesday. I look up at its big brown fins and watch it spin, just enough to move the smells of us through the room: my perfume, his cologne, fabric softener, the food we like, Allie's kibble.

My boxes are stacked in a high tan castle in the living room where the carpet is the color of hamburger. We spent a hundred nights sitting tense on the edge of the couch, drumming our fingers on the table, pacing the burger carpet, trying to understand why I wanted to leave the man I'd always wanted. We tried waiting it out and talking it out and praying it out. We bought a dog. We bought a black teddy from the Victoria's Secret catalog. We bought red wine. Nothing helped. We hoped, fervently, desperately, madly:

Maybe things will be better when we move back to Texas?

Maybe I need a better support system?

Maybe I need to be a better support system? He works so damn hard. He's trying so damn hard.

Maybe I'll wake up and feel different tomorrow?

Maybe I could get the fake boobs he'd suggested that one time and immediately regretted suggesting?

Maybe we could get another dog?

But the one dog didn't help at all. And she's a Great Dane.

We also tried yelling at each other but that didn't work. We've never really been able to fight. We like each other enough to let some things go but don't love each other enough to hold on to the ones that matter.

For a while we thought we could be on different pages, just so long as we kept doing things by the book: She will be a nurse. He will be a surgeon. They will have beautiful towheaded babies. She will stay home with the kids. He will have a career. They will be faithful and kind to each other. They will move back to Texas. It will be enough.

But it wasn't, isn't, and won't be. Not for me. If you do things by the book, you miss out on your own story. I don't want either of us to miss another second.

I take my shoes off and stand barefoot in the middle of the room and breathe the last of us in, not sure whether I'm trying to remember or forget him.

"Do you want us to put these on the truck, ma'am?" One of the boys is standing at the threshold, still super excited, still reeling from the energy drinks.

"Sure. And you can call me Mary." I smile. I'm wearing jean shorts; let's not "ma'am" the divorcée while she's down.

He runs back to the truck and, for a reason only teenage boys can explain, they high-five and begin hauling boxes.

Allie, our dog, *my* dog now, is in the guest bedroom yipping and batting at the doorknob. She moved out of the master when I did and hasn't been back since, not even for a sniff. She's a hundred-pound slinky when I open the door, wiggling and bouncing and flicking my hands with her nose. I give her a kiss and she follows me into our old bedroom across the hall to give the closet a check.

The bed is made, which used to be my job, and there's still a picture of us on the bedstand, a reminder that I'm leaving, that I gave up, that he would have kept trying. Our faces are pressed close together and we're smiling. Fruitlessly, I wonder what changed, knowing quietly in my heart that I did.

The closet is wide-open and it looks like a tomb without my things in it, without the shoes and the dresses, the big sleeves and brash, cheeky prints that made him blush when we were at dinner.

"Maybe something a little understated?" he would suggest as gently as he could.

My style evolved. I started dressing differently and he didn't understand. I started thinking differently and he didn't understand. I fell in love with flouncy things and color-blocked things, things that made my belly flip. I began reading *Women's Wear Daily* as much with my imagination as my eyes. I started writing and never wanted to stop. I created *Happily Grey,* a place I could run wild, share, explore. It became my job, my passion, my home, and he didn't understand. Dreams came, *new* dreams, and new dreams were never a part of the plan. The plan was med school Ken and nurse Barbie. It wasn't his fault. Like him, I loved the plan . . . until I met the dream. We tried and tried, me hoping he would change, him hoping just as hard that I wouldn't. He couldn't understand, even though he wanted to.

The idea of divorce broke him when I said it out loud. "You were supposed to be a nurse and then . . . you . . . were supposed to be a stay-at-home mom." The words shook out of him, the two of us seated next to each other on the floor staring into space.

"I know. I'm sorry," I whispered, holding his beautiful, sad face, gathering the stuff to meet the steady hazel eyes that anchored me on our wedding day. I really was sorry. I *am* sorry.

Allie pulls me from the memory, nudging my hand with her nose and spinning in the smallest circles she can make with her cow-spotted Cadillac of a body. Together we go back into the living room to check in on the movers.

"Everything's set with boxes, ma'am," the really-skinny tall boy says. "Any of this furniture coming?"

I look around the room at the lamps and side tables, the chaise lounge, and the big television where he used to watch Longhorns football and I used to pretend to like it. We'd talked about the furniture some, but he'd just told me to take whatever I needed. My brain spins.

I don't know.

I want nothing and everything.

I wish my mom was here.

I wish my friends were here.

I wish he was here.

We tried our best. I swear it.

The boy waits on the stoop and shifts his weight a little. "Ma'am?"

I decide to just give up on the "ma'am" thing. I'll be Ma'am today. "Yeah, hold on. I just need a second."

Obediently, he wanders back to the truck to chest-bump his friend and play on his phone.

I stare down the living room and try to divide the only assets we have: a couch, a coffee table, random decor. I try to think about all of it objectively, detaching each little trinket from its history, not allowing myself to return to the night we moved in and danced together across the stiff brown floor. The tears come, but I don't let myself break down. I wave the boys back in and rattle off instructions.

Take the white leather sofa.

Leave the high-back chair that held me in its squeaky leather arms while I learned to write.

Take the side table with magazines.

Leave the kitchen table where I told him I wasn't in love with him anymore.

They load the truck, pull down the string, and it's done. They drive off to my new equally brown apartment just a few miles down the road. It's just me, Allie, and half a living room, shadows of an older, fuller life pressed deep into the carpet.

"He can't come home to this," I tell Allie, who isn't sure she agrees and gives her tail a noncommittal shrug of a wag.

First, I move the coffee table closer to the chair. Then I angle the lamp so it doesn't shine on the space where the couch used to be. The TV moves forward about a foot and the side table gets a squirt of Pledge and a quick polish. I shake out the curtains, rehang the art, and sweep, until every last dust bunny and gum wrapper has been lifted from the floor.

Just before I go, I turn off the light and slide a copy of *Women's Wear Daily* onto the table, hoping with all my heart that he finds what I did: something that turns the world a brighter color, a good story, a dream. At the last second, I swap the magazine out with a Victoria's Secret catalog. I think he'll find something he likes there.

Keep SAKES

Living Room

He was everything I'd ever wanted—kind, faithful, ambitious, a lover of Jesus and Texas, an owner of golf clubs and good suits, handsome as the off-brand Ken doll I paraded around my childhood bedroom with Totally Hair Barbie. He said the right things and made the right choices, rarely ever putting a foot wrong. I fell in love with the steadfastness and consistency, the ability to form and stick to a plan. He never, ever changed, but then I did.

At about eighteen, I got it into my head that I was complete. I had grown up and, therefore, was done growing entirely. Boy, I was wrong. At thirty-four, I'm just getting started. One of the great joys of my adult life has been meeting my inner child, watching myself grow, surprising myself, changing my plans, falling flat on my face, getting up, choosing the unknown, and relishing in the wide, wonderful freedom to become. My ex and I were hard-nosed enough that we could have loved each other for a lifetime, but we would have missed out on knowing and loving ourselves. We would have stopped changing and that would have been the true heartbreak.

We would have stopped changing and that would have been the true heartbreak.

Fleetwood Mac Songs

(That Also Happen to Be Genius Self-Love Practices)

Even though I did the big, brave, "turn the world upside down and get a divorce" thing, I was still a bit of a baby afterward. I didn't have family or friends nearby. I was working by myself. Nashville didn't even have a Nordstrom yet. For about a month all I did was listen to Fleetwood Mac, take bubble baths, and cry softly into Allie's neck fur.

Maybe it's because I was entering an exploratory phase with seventies fringe, or maybe it's because they know a thing or two about breakups, but lovesickness and Fleetwood Mac just felt right together. The music was familiar when hardly anything else was. Plus, taking a spin on their emotional roller coaster made mine feel more manageable, like an emotional Tilt-A-Whirl maybe.

If you've even a crumb of grief in your heart, my number one piece of advice is to download Fleetwood Mac's entire catalog. After that, spend time loving on yourself. If you don't know where to start, give these practices (and heart-melting tracks) a spin!

"GO YOUR OWN WAY"

I'd never really had my own life before. I was a daughter, and then I was a wife. I was a kid playing with dolls, and then I was a nurse caring for patients. I was a rule follower and people pleaser to the absolute max. After the divorce, for the first time ever, I made my own rules. Don't worry, I didn't go topless at the Home Depot or drive seventy past a school or anything.

Instead of arranging my new kitchen the way my mom would have done it, or my husband would have liked it, I went my own damn way. Instead of having a closet for guests, I took all the closets. Instead of buying a toaster, I bought lipstick. Through those busy, blurry first days, it helped to pause and quietly remind myself that I had permission to do things that made me feel good.

"DON'T STOP"

Some people are great at sitting still in their pain and feeling it all, but I am not one of those people, though sitting still is a wise, beautiful, highly evolved action. For me, staying busy was key to staying healthy. I kept my calendar and my heart full. Traveling to different cities, meeting new people, sinking myself into projects I cared about kept life purposeful, peaceful, and pretty damn exciting, even in the midst of sadness.

"SENTIMENTAL LADY"

Happily remarried now with two kids, I *still* have moments where I grieve the failure of a marriage and feel the disappointment of my family members and *myself*. Divorce was 4000 percent the right thing and the best thing, and also 4000 percent harder than anything else I'd ever done before. I have no regrets; that time in the romantic trenches led to a world of growth and made me the woman I am today. But it was deeply painful—for him, for me, and for our families. Even as an echo, the ache is still very real. For a long time after I'd moved on, I told myself that I wasn't allowed to be sad anymore—but I was allowed, I am allowed, and so are you. Be gentle with yourself, sob, eat macaroni, and know it may always feel a bit sad and that's okay.

"THINK ABOUT ME"

You already know there was some soaking in the tub. What you don't know is that this was high-performance, next-level, double-black-belt self-care. After the end of my relationship, I was depleted. All I wanted was to be held, but for the first time in my adult life, there was nobody there to do it. I had to find a way all on my own, so I went full Nicholas Sparks and wooed myself silly. For thirty consecutive nights, my bathroom looked more honeymoon than divorce. I pulled out all the stops—wine, dark chocolate, a sixty-dollar candle that smelled like the ocean. I rediscovered what it was not just to treat myself but to show myself true care and compassion.

"SHAKE YOUR MONEYMAKER"

Or play chess or hike or sing! Do whatever it is that brings laughter to your belly and leaves you breathless. For me, it was dancing my heart away at the 5 Spot on Motown Mondays. Follow the endorphins.

Easy Living

If the kitchen is the heart of a house, the living room is the soul. It's where the fire pops and spits and where Santa Claus leaves the presents. It's where the glasses of wine are poured and the feet are put up to rest at the end of the day. The living room is where children pull their doughy little bodies up and cruise along the furniture, taking time to adorn the glass coffee table with crumbs and prints from their squishy palms. Simply and aptly, the living room is where life happens.

But sometimes, life is overwhelming.

Designing such a hallowed space can be intimidating, but the good news is that there are no hard rules. I've felt at home in stark, modern spaces and velvety vintage ones, but I've also felt *not* at home, and normally it has nothing to do with aesthetics and everything to do with ease of use. When configuring a space, keep comfort and common sense at the forefront with these dos and *maybe* don'ts.

MAYBE DON'T push your furniture up against the wall. I don't know why we do it, but we do, and there's nothing worse than stretching out your legs for that coffee table and coming up short. **DO** come together! Create an intimate space where everybody is close enough to talk *and* put their feet up.

MAYBE DON'T skimp on the seating. If you're an entertainer or mama of a megabrood, splurge on the sectional—don't squeeze onto the love seat. **DO** have a few comfortable stand-alone chairs around the house that you can move easily when extra guests come over to play.

LR

Interior designer Lindsay Rhodes has an unparalleled ability to transform your space into a cohesive and distinctive dwelling. Based in Nashville, Tennessee, Lindsay has spent the past fifteen years honing her process to yield spaces that uniquely reflect each individual client. "No design looks the same because no person is the same," explains Lindsay.

MAYBE DON'T design the room around your television. I like an NFL Sunday as much as the rest of 'em, but a good living room should direct focus to the people in your space, not to your screen. **DO** invest in art pieces and accessories you love to spark conversation.

MAYBE DON'T be too trendy. If you ride the Southwest-inspired train too hard, it'll take you straight to Tombstone. Say it with one or two Navajo print pillows, not seven. But **DO** allow yourself one totally crazy chair.

MAYBE DON'T go all high-maintenance. Ideally, you'll spend more time living in your living room than cleaning it. If you've got pets and littles, try not to fall in love with that white sofa or flat paint. If you're planning to play hostess a lot, go for an easy-to-vacuum low-pile rug instead of shag. **DO** buy a robot vacuum. Seriously. Right now. Alternatively, if you're more the hands-on type and like the idea of driving a Ferrari through your living room, invest in a Dyson.

MAYBE DON'T make it posh. An overly stark, anesthetized room feels more like a waiting area than a living area. Err on the side of warm and welcoming. **DO** make it personal. Add frames to those preschool Picassos! Show off your family photos! Line the shelves with your grandfather's field guides and your mom's Nancy Drews.

MAYBE DON'T get cluttered. Living in your living room means that sometimes, things will get messy. Magazines will stack up, toys and tech will migrate, snacks will sidle on in. **DO** get sneaky with storage. Designers have wised up. Plenty of side tables, coffee tables, and ottomans (ottomen?) moonlight as toy trunks, blanket boxes, and treasure chests. Stash away, sister!

Green Goddess

I'm never sure if I need another baby, but I'm always sure that I need another plant. Adding green to your scene brings beautiful layers of texture and color, cleaner indoor air, and an extra bit of life and brightness that not even the fanciest floor lamp can rival. When I left my ex-husband and holed up at the Four Seasons condo complex (very different from the hotel, I assure you), it was just me, Allie, and a snake plant I bought at Kroger. It wasn't the healthiest plant (and I did it no favors at all), but it sat with me in my brand-new space and served as a daily reminder to grow, which—against the odds—both of us did.

I love all the little plant children from Aloe to ZZ, but these beauties take my breath away.

ALOCASIA

I don't like to pick favorites, but alocasia, you've stolen my whole heart. The leaf shape! The deep, deep greens and white, white veins! The sheen! She's a little finicky when it comes to light (bright) and humidity (high), but she sure is pretty.

ALOE

Easy, nontoxic, filled with healing goo, and perfect for bookshelves and desktops.

ARBEQUINA OLIVE TREE

Longing for Italy? I am! At all times! With beautiful grey-green foliage and a long, lanky trunk, olive trees work wonderfully with modern, *sunny* interiors. You may even end up with some fruit.

BISHOP'S CAP CACTUS

You had me at "water infrequently." For a low-maintenance, high-impact plant for your desk or window ledge, it doesn't get better. Just watch your fingers!

BURGUNDY RUBBER TREE

Deep greens, rich reds, waxy leaves you could use as hand mirrors—what's not to love? You can keep it small to midsize in a little pot or give it more room and watch it grow as tall as you are.

BURRO'S TAIL

Place your burro's tail on a high shelf or a hanging planter to take full advantage of its dramatic, waterfalling foliage.

PONYTAIL PALM

Just try not to smile at this wacky guy. Believe it or not, ponytail palms are actually succulents, and aside from a little sunshine and light water, they don't need much from you care-wise.

WATERMELON PEPEROMIA

Has anything ever scored such high points in the Sheer Adorableness category? I think not! In exchange for its cuteness, the watermelon peperomia doesn't need much from you: not a ton of watering, not a ton of sun, just a decent-sized pot and a place where it can be fawned over.

CHAPTER 6

Jets Over London

Curiosity is a good leader.

I'm not far from Covent Garden when I see the jets appear out of the corner of my eye. There are nine of them in a giant *V*, screaming through the afternoon sky like an angry gang of titanium geese. I blink a few times and try to shake the delirium and jet lag from my head. I've never traveled outside the United States before, and I stayed up all night on the plane talking to a nice, older man about everything from medieval history to my divorce to the consistency of the tortellini they gave us for dinner. We hoped it was cheese in the middle but neither of us could say for certain.

The planes roar a little closer.

I don't know what's happening but everyone around me is relaxed, so I relax too. The people at the sidewalk cafés look up fondly from their foamy dark pints and return to their conversations. A group of shoppers give the planes a quick glance but seem much more interested in the thin, headless mannequins in the Zara window display. Chatter I collect but only half understand from a man buying gum at the newsstand tells me that it's the queen's birthday today. That's what the jets are for. I guess a Carvel ice cream cake wouldn't cut it. I keep staring, totally mystified, looking straight up.

When the jets hit the exact middle of the sky, each releases a bright, dusty tail of pigment. Mile-long plumes of scarlet, ivory, and cornflower blue burst through the air and hang lazily next to the clouds. Just in time, I liberate my phone from the ridiculous travel belt I'd bought and snap a photo before the colors slowly, almost hesitantly, meet to become purple.

The picture is absolutely

perfect. It's been a long time since I've taken a photo that wasn't carefully planned, styled, and staged, illuminated with a weird circle-shaped light that makes everything it touches look ten years younger (even shoes). But this one I netted like a butterfly. The nine planes are arranged just as they should be in the frame, crossing over a flat-roofed building with a vivid tricolor wake.

I'm in London for work. I have thirty meetings scheduled all around town over the next nine days and no idea how the Tube works, which I'm certain will turn out wonderfully for everyone. *Happily Grey* is growing faster than I ever thought it would. People all over the world read the internet like it's the daily paper now and somehow, we've Pinterested our way to the fashion section. I'm also here because I've never been far away before. I've never even eaten different food or not understood what somebody was saying to me. I've never let myself get lost before. I've never really been on my own before. Now I'm just Mary, four thousand miles from home.

London isn't the most enormous cultural leap, but the aloneness is. Everything around me is unfamiliar, from the nakedness of my ring finger to the skinny streets that sway through the city. With no one waiting for me at home, I can wander as long as I like. With no conversation to keep up with, I can listen—to the round-bellied pigeon flapping as hard as she can to protect her precious french fry, to the busker singing "Friday I'm in Love." The current of the foot traffic on the pavement carries me along past baroque buildings guarded by gilded lions, iron gates, and sneering gargoyles, past a stone William Shakespeare standing awkwardly in the center of a fountain, past big red buses rushing around Piccadilly like they're about to tip over. Miraculously, I find my Airbnb and collapse onto the couch as soon as I get in. I'm too excited to get any good sleep though.

Curiosity is a good leader, and over the next few days I let mine lead me. I go for long morning runs at Hyde Park, stopping underneath the marble arch and saying hello just because I want to know if my voice will come back to me under the soft white curve. It doesn't. I learn the names of the roses in the garden and trace their elegant spindly branches, tapping the end of a thorn with my index finger to see if it'll hurt. It does. I sit on a bench at Serpentine Lake watching mandarin ducks float across the smooth surface, making hardly a ripple on the water, feathers looking like they were painted with fine, careful brushstrokes and lacquered so they would shine like the black cabs do. I absorb the fashion, which is totally different from Nashville. Even though it's June, nobody is wearing flip-flops and I see flashes of tweed, just like I hoped I would. A satisfying amount of people look like they could try out for Sgt. Pepper's Lonely Hearts Club Band.

A lot of questions come up. Most of them, I'm too embarrassed to ask.

How long did it take to build the Tower Bridge?

What's the difference between a church and an abbey?

Does anybody like this tea?

Where's the toilet?

And I have questions for myself too. I chew on them as I go along, getting turned around again and again:

Why did you get married?

Did you ever really love him?

What do you want to do with your life?

What are you really doing here?

I grew up in a world that had all the answers: black and white, right and wrong, good and bad, what was possible and what wasn't. Somewhere along the way, I stopped asking questions. I forgot how to be curious. I started shrinking from joy and calling it silly. I thought I knew everything, but alone, in a strange city with crisp air and new words, there

is so much more freedom in not knowing. That's what *Happily Grey* is all about. It's a return to wonder, to joy, to the thrill of uncertainty.

A schoolyard lets out in Notting Hill one afternoon and it's a fit of giggles, freckled cheeks, and tartan. The students move around me like I'm a fence post stuck in the middle of the stark white streets. I'm too grown up and inanimate for them to notice, unable to speak their magic language of spitballs and jump rope. I look at them and feel the ecstasy of the school bell ringing at 3 p.m. I feel the liberty of nine years old. I remember the soft earth under my feet, the freckles on my own cheeks, and what it was to play. Something that had gone long ago falls back into place and the questions I used to ask return to me:

Why do the cows lie down before it rains?

Will I ever catch a big fish?

Some questions are still the same:

What does love feel like?

I have a shoot the next day and for the first time, I plan nothing and feel everything instead. I become nine again and play in my pink balletic skirt all the way down Portobello Road. I twirl, twirl, twirl and lose myself in the folds of the fabric, watching it move around my calves like knee-deep creek water. I laugh from the deepest part of my belly and let my hair fall down. For the rest of the week, I absorb as much of the world as I can and I use it, painting my lips double-decker-bus red and choosing a dress as white as swan feathers. I stand in stony stillness like Shakespeare in the middle of his fountain (but not quite as awkwardly) and rush forward like a jet plane.

The end of each day is still jarring. At 10:30 p.m., I come home to no one. Things are dark, quiet, and exactly as I left them. It shouldn't be a surprise anymore, but it is. The stale, warm air of the old building hangs heavy, so I open the windows and invite the city inside: petrol and late-night kebab, drunken laughter and football songs. I curl my body into a chair near the window and watch, saying a slow goodbye to all of it, knowing that soon, I'll be gone from this magical place.

The asphalt outside is a whole new shimmering sky under the streetlamps, and in one synchronized movement, the pubs let out. Oily, nebulous puddles spin and shine in a dozen ways until a careless shoe turns everything to brown. The lingerers find the last drops in their glasses and couples, new and old, pair off from the crowds to go home, occasionally stopping to kiss sloppily against one of the long-clawed gargoyles. A few try fruitlessly to find a cab brave enough to drive them. As they wobble and collapse into each other's arms, kissing while everyone watches, stumbling while everyone watches, I wonder what it feels like. I know I've never felt it before. A pint glass cracks against the pavement and shatters into a thousand sparkling pieces. Somebody cusses in the street and I smile at the horrible, foul word.

Just before I fall asleep in the small, firm bed, I grab my phone and look back at the jets in the sky, cutting through the dull grey clouds and setting their colors loose. I touch my fingers to the screen, tracing the blue, then the white, then the red, knowing that they weren't my last surprise, feeling comforted by the unknown instead of frightened by it. Sleep comes quickly, lulled on by the beat of my own heart, the steady rush of a two-thousand-year-old city, and the wonder of tomorrow.

Keep SAKES

Jets *Over London*

If curiosity killed the cat, she died happy. Crossing the ocean for the first time awakened me, romanced me, and reminded me just how little of the world I knew. Tricolor jets overhead, four-hundred-year-old gargoyles on the stoop, and clotted cream in my belly, I was smitten: with London, and with travel, sunk deep into the study of the people and places. For just shy of two weeks, with sweaty palms and a fluttering heart, I walked and walked, taking everything and everyone in, collapsing into bed at the end of the day with messy hair, sore feet, and my hand at my heart. Some people call it wanderlust. I call it love.

Some people call it wanderlust. I call it love.

Details

I stayed in Covent Garden, right down the street from St. Paul's Church, an enormous red-brick temple with a grand portico smack in the middle of the city. Even though I'd grown up in churches, for the first few days I just wandered by St. Paul's, unsure if I was allowed to just pop into a seventeenth-century architectural masterpiece or whether it was off-limits to curious, common Americans. Turns out, anyone can go in. I don't even think the door (which is about twenty feet tall) has a lock.

The familiar fusty smell of worship, old ink, and mildew hit me as soon as I walked inside, but everything else was different. All of it, from the pipe organ to the pews, was art. The arched windows cast jewel-colored beams of light onto my face as I walked toward the lectern, taking in each stitch of the gilded brocade behind the pulpit and every little curl of the lovingly carved wood. The arms of the clock, the folds of Mary's knuckle, the long bronze branches of the chandeliers—it was all exquisite, not a single detail overlooked. Now I look for the details everywhere.

A Very British Closet

Before I touched down at Heathrow, I wasn't clued in to London's sophisticated street style at all. I was hoping that everybody would either look like a Beefeater or a Spice Girl, but alas, most Brits seemed to land somewhere in between. There was no athleisure (a shock to my Lycra-clad American system) and everyone looked polished, even if they were tumbling out of the pub toward the chip shop. I learned a ton about what basics you really need to get by. You can't condense an entire cosmopolitan culture down to a few measly items of clothing, but after my time in the UK my closet will always contain the following:

TRENCH COAT

A trench coat is never wrong. Whether you're chasing after the garbage truck with your trash cans barefoot (and possibly bare-arsed) at 7 a.m. or headed to a meeting, a trench coat is light, flattering, and professional, easy to wear and easy to love.

CHELSEA BOOTS

As much as I love a pair of Wellies, the Chelsea boot can stand up to sloppy, soupy UK weather and big-city style. I wear mine with everything from a mini (more on that later) to the Salvation Army cutoffs I (still) make every April. There aren't a lot of footwear choices in this world that can take you from a work meeting to a music festival, but the Chelsea boot is made for walking pretty much anywhere.

TWEED

I wait all summer for tweed time. It's cozy, sturdy, and it goes with literally everything. I'll wear it with silk, and I'll wear it with leather. I'll pair it with a blouse or a concert tee.

NEWSBOY CAP

Why wear a beanie when you can be *extra*? Sorry, I had to. Seriously though, as far as hats go, the newsboy is fairly democratic. It looks great on everyone, it's warm, and it offers a little more fancy than a stinky old skullcap.

PETER PAN COLLAR

Wild, whimsical, and so very Wendy, there are few things that capture my imagination like a Kate Middleton meets James Barrie fashion extravaganza. A Peter Pan collar is an easy way to dress up without *really* dressing up.

MINISKIRT

Just when you thought it was going to be all stiff, neutral fabrics and no play, behold! The *mini*! The miniskirt was a sixties London staple and I'm not sure that anything else, at least in that era, made such a mark on women's streetwear. Coco Chanel allegedly hated them, but everybody else was having too much fun to care!

CHAPTER 7
Plane Tickets

I don't love him because he makes me feel safe—
I love him because he makes me feel free.

I thought I knew what love was, but I was wrong. I don't like being wrong. I spend three years after my divorce trying to understand how it all fell apart, what was missing, and why it was gone, but none of it makes sense to me.

Friends marry. They have one fat little baby they're wild about, and then they have more. None of them seem to be able to put the feeling of it all into words and I do not ask them to try. With burp rags on their shoulders and glassy eyes, my sisters and friends attempt to map love out for me like the choreographed dance I want it to be, but everybody's steps are different. All anyone can say for sure is that when you know, you know.

Madison is from Shreveport; I can tell in an instant. I know what home sounds like, whether I'm watching cows with my brother on my family's farm or drinking the five-dollar vodka sodas in a dive off Music Row. It's December 2016. My agent, Emily, and I are in Midtown at an after-party for a charity event where nearly everybody was wearing too

much perfume and under thirty years old. The bar we're at is a beloved institution, weird and wonderful with music a few decibels too loud and a design story that consists entirely of plastic skeletons and the Chicago Cubs. I'm totally here for it and, judging by the laughter pouring onto the patio, so is everyone else.

We set up outside for a moment under a heat lamp that smells like burnt hair and propane but decide to go in when the flame gets too blue and too hot. A swell of drunken banter and nineties grunge swallows us up when we step into the barroom. We say hello to the other good-smelling young people and head toward the bar, a trek in which Emily is lost to a conversation with a fellow agent about a random concert venue. I'm happy to drift and listen to the music, a blur of distorted guitars, cymbals, and impossible-to-decipher lyrics. Eventually I land in the light of the Budweiser sign and grab onto the bar like it's the ledge of a swimming pool, making a space for myself between oblivious arms and elbows. The bartender catches my eye and tips an invisible glass to her lips. *Just a single*, I tell her with my index finger. She grabs the gin and goes to work.

While I wait, in a soup of arguments and stories and jokes and Nirvana, I hear something familiar, some *place* familiar. I stare out into the forest of people and their sweaty clothes and hear it again, getting closer, sounding more and more like home—the Red

River, the big sky, Caddo Lake, crawfish tails, and football. Just as I wrap my fingers around the wet, generic bar glass, he's right next to me.

"Hey, Mary." He smiles.

We've met before. His name is Madison. The last time I saw him we were both tipsy, hoarse, and probably had sunstroke from an afternoon talking over music at an outdoor festival. He works with Emily at Creative Artists Agency. I couldn't really hear much of his voice then, but I hear it now. It's deep and sexy but speckled with familiar little mannerisms, lilts, and pauses and syllables drawn all the way out. I feel like I'm at home with him.

"Where are you from?" I ask when he's about three sentences in, feeling more confident than I usually do and chewing on the end of my cocktail straw.

"Shreveport, Louisiana," he says.

"I knew it! What hospital were you born in?"

It's a weird question but he doesn't seem put off by it. "Willis-Knighton South, I think." He grins. "You too?" We grew up less than twenty miles from each other.

I nod in an excited way, not a cool one. *Shit, Mary. Why did you ask him that?!*

Madison smiles and it washes the whole world away. The music is gone. The people with their chicken wings and cigarettes are gone. We sit at the bar, which is adorned with

a million spare pennies under a sheet of scratched plexiglass, and we talk. It's just the two of us and it stays that way.

We spend every possible moment of the next five days together, not really dating but quietly processing the impossible but totally undeniable reality of loving each other. On day one, winter comes in earnest, so we sit in the early darkness drinking white wine and creeping closer and closer together, talking about everything—growing up, the church, how many kids we want and when we want them. On day two, he orders four drinks for himself at breakfast—coffee, juice, water, and a mimosa—and I notice how kind he is to strangers on the street. On day three, he asks me six thousand questions. What was my favorite song in high school? Do I like to be the tiny dog or the thimble in Monopoly? Where do I want to travel next in the world and why?

I say Cuba. It's the last one on my bucket list for the year.

"Let's go one day." He smiles, and I melt.

Day four is almost entirely melting.

I imagine that things will fall into a pattern for us and I'll like it when they do—I'll feel safer. We're moving too fast and neither of us has the wherewithal to take a single step back. We're kissing on the street and falling into each other. We're talking about children and international travel. If there were patterns, there could be predictions, and then there could be plans. I could troubleshoot, and if I could troubleshoot, I could solve all of our problems before they problemed themselves into existence. Nobody would get hurt. Nobody would get divorced. We would meet families at the correct time, exchange house keys at the correct time. But Mad isn't much of a patterns guy and he's unafraid of love. On day five, I count him say "I love" five times: to his friends, his UPS guy, his niece, Phoenix, and twice to the Nashville Predators.

On day six, it starts snowing on Thursday morning while I'm at work. We're in the middle of the holiday rush and I've got two weeks' worth of content to write. I haven't stood still since I woke up, but I stop to watch the little crystals tumble down and melt on the warm, brown grass because it will always be magic to me.

My phone buzzes in my pocket. It's Mad. No message, just an attachment.

Two Southwest flights to Havana. Leaving in less than a week.

We're not ready; I'm not ready. It doesn't make sense, but I look down at the staggering perfection of our names seated next to each other in print and wonder if it needs to.

The buildings in Old Havana are as curvy as the streets and all painted in shades of saltwater taffy. They rise from the cobblestone with great domed roofs, Juliet balconies, and scalloped shingles, and stare out at the slate-colored sea. We spend the first morning walking, taking photos of the old Buicks and Studebakers parked at the pier, shimmering in the sun while cabbies polish, polish, polish, and try to pick up their next fare. There's no Wi-Fi, no American dollar, no weird digital rat race to run. Nobody knows what *Happily Grey* is, and from what I can tell, nobody really cares. All I am here is myself. Another person falling in love, letting the skinny alleyways lead them under clotheslines that drip, past men in pleated pants playing dominoes, over piles of fruit skin rotting in the sun.

I've traveled at least forty times more extensively than Mad but he's fifty times more prepared than I am. He showed up to the airport with $750 worth of Cuban pesos, a travel

guide, and a few mouthfuls of passable Spanish. I showed up with a bunch of bikinis and good shoes. The whole flight, I assured him I'd change money when we landed, not remembering that the Cuban government is about as interested in my American Express as they are in my Instagram account. He'd nicely told me during our layover in Tampa that I probably wouldn't have much luck banking in Havana. I decided to ignore him. So now we are on a communist dream vacation with hardly any money. And it's my fault.

"I'm so sorry," I tell him over and over, as a little old lady and her studious cat show off heaps of plantain, papaya, and spiky green soursop, which neither of us has seen before.

"We'll get by." Mad smiles, slinging an arm around my waist and moving onward.

With all the excitement in the world, the woman hands us one of the strange, spiny, football-shaped fruits and a machete, but we pass. The mangoes are cheaper and we're on a budget.

Mad doesn't seem to care at all that we're pinching pesos. He's going with the flow, even if secretly he doesn't want to. We spend the next days on simple, wonderful, cheap things—fresh muddled mint and white rum that burns our throats, giant churros from stalls on the street, strangely delicious pork hamburgers with pineapple rings on top. We pass modern restaurants with craft cocktails, upscale boutiques, and contemporary galleries, but quickly release any longings we might have for crudo or wine served at the correct temperature. We hang out at La Bodeguita del Medio instead, a little bar under a mustard-colored sign with free music where you can sign your name on the wall and promise yourself you'll come back to see it one day. We dance (badly) to Afro-Cuban jazz played on wood blocks, congas, and nylon-stringed guitars, and wonder if this bar really is *the* bar where Hemingway went for mojitos. I've never had less or been happier.

Mad talks to anyone and everyone. He wants to know about the spiky green fruits, why Cuban dominoes are different from American ones, and how they make the tostones so good. We spend two joyful hours one day just wondering about the different kinds of moss growing on the sides of the buildings and tossing cubes of bread to the gulls who live by the water and are already too well-fed to fly. I don't check the time or my email or worry about anything other than fat birds getting too fat on plantain and dying. Mostly, I lean my salt-kissed head on Mad's shoulder and marvel—at the cracks in the road, the street art, and how free I am.

When he falls asleep at night in our sweet pink-walled rental, I lay awake a bit longer and whisper almost inaudibly that I love him, that I have been loving him almost every second since we met. I love him when he's drinking his guava smoothie and when he's asking yet another person yet another question. I love that we have no money and that he doesn't care and that the most exciting thing in the world to him is sitting down on a bench near the barnacle-covered boats and talking to me. I don't love him because he makes me feel safe—I love him because he makes me feel free. I'm more curious when I'm with him. I ask more questions, I look deeper, and I laugh harder. By day five, I'm using the word *love* more freely than I normally do, even though it feels cheesy. I love the buildings and the churros and the briny smell of the pier. I love white rum and bad dancing. I love Mad, too, but I don't tell him just yet.

I watch six hot-orange sunsets with my head on his chest and listen, equally as enamored by the beat of his heart and the rumble of his belly as I am with the sky. We're the only two people on earth to lose weight on vacation. When we get back to Nashville, he tells me that he loves me, and he doesn't stop. He tells me in Chattanooga when we're walking beside the Tennessee River. He tells me in Copenhagen after seven months together and puts a ring on my finger. A month shy of our one-year anniversary, he tells me at Bloomsbury Farm in a tux in front of our friends and family, while our flower girls run barefoot through the long grass and pick white violets.

I know less and less about the world as it unfolds before us bigger and more beautifully than I ever could have dreamed. I'm less sure of what's true in the world but more and more in awe of it. The one thing I do know, though, is what love is. But I'll never, ever be able to explain it.

Keep SAKES

Plane Tickets

Officially, I can't recommend international travel within the first month of a romantic relationship. Unofficially, it's awesome and we had the best time. Even though we hardly knew each other and ran out of money after three and a half days. At one point, since our American Express cards were no good to Raúl Castro, I actually had to call a British ex-boyfriend and have him wire us some cash, which was exactly as awkward as it sounds. For all of us. Mad and I were stranded at a hotel in Varadero and didn't have enough money to pay for our lunch or the cab back to Havana. Desperate times call for desperate measures.

The situation wasn't ideal, but we learned how to pinch our pesos *and* have a hell of a lot of fun doing it. Even though I don't always feel swept up and romantic about it, we still try to stick to a budget when we're on the road these days, especially with kids in tow. Here are just a few things we do to keep costs at bay.

Big love, little budget.

WALK. EVERYWHERE.

If you're staying somewhere safe, walking will save you some serious cash and help you burn off those foot-long churros. For us, it's the best way to explore a new place, meet people, and find the dive bar we want to hit at happy hour. Speaking of . . .

HIT HAPPY HOUR

After 6 p.m., the whole world becomes twenty American dollars more expensive. Take advantage of the miser's golden hour and get yourself some bargain wines and two-dollar tapas. Nothing stings the next day like a ribeye hangover and a hole in your pocket.

SAY YES TO STREET FOOD

Whether it's micheladas in Mexico, Chicago dogs, or *bakso* in Bali, street food just tastes better than other food *and* it's budget friendly. I'm not saying don't splurge on a fancy meal one night, but I bet as you slide into that leather booth a part of you will long to be standing at a food stall, waiting, smelling, and listening. Since we're on the topic of street things . . .

SAY YES TO STREET ART TOO!

I love a good peruse in a good gallery, but nothing beats the energy, brightness, and price of street art. Ask your Airbnb host or new bartender pal for a list of favorite murals, or wander until you stumble upon them yourself.

KEEP CALM, CARRY ON

Don't worry, I'm just talking about your luggage. I do not travel light, but oh, do I long to! If you can live without all the shoes, all the jewelry, all the hats, and way too many bags, do it. I can't, but I beg of you to carry on your luggage and carry on with your life. While you're sinking your toes into sand and sipping your first daiquiri, I'll still be over at baggage claim praying they didn't send my Marant sweater to Vancouver instead of Varadero.

DRINK LOCAL!

In general, local beers and liquors are going to be cheaper than your go-to imported swill. Try something new and save enough to tip your bartender.

Cuba? *Really?*

Yes, Cuba! And Slovenia and Laos and Honduras and Lichtenstein! Not-so-obvious destinations are my absolute favorite, and I still keep a travel bucket list that I'm determined to plow my way through by fifty (but if Mad buys me a ticket to Montevideo tomorrow, I probably can't make it this weekend). Here are my top twelve:

Not-so-obvious destinations are my absolute favorite.

CROATIA

Truffles, wine, beautiful seascapes, good weather, the smallest city in the world . . . (Seriously! It's called Hum.) What's not to love?

BHUTAN

Bhutan is harder to get into than Harvard Law, but I don't blame them. This Buddhist kingdom nestled in the Himalayas stayed nearly unknown to the rest of us until the 1970s and it looks absolutely breathtaking. Fun fact: it's the only carbon-negative nation in the world.

URUGUAY

Little country, big wine producer, sign me up! Uruguay is also socially progressive, home to a stunning coastline, and knows what to do with a steak.

BOTSWANA

When I read online that nearly 40 percent of the land in Botswana was protected to preserve the nation's (totally incredible and bonkers) wildlife, I was in. Botswana has salt flats, river deltas, the Kalahari Desert, and more elephants than anywhere else in the world!

CHILE

Patagonia! Easter Island! Vineyards! Vistas! Villas! Volcanoes! For a smallish country, there sure is *a lot* to see.

TURKEY

I'm a sucker for an archaeological wonder and Turkey has a whopping nineteen UNESCO World Heritage sites, including the Rock Sites of Cappadocia, Troy, and Ephesus.

OMAN

Westerners who are hesitant to visit the Middle East should know that Oman scores a zero on the Global Terrorism Index. It may be quieter than its flashier, more popular neighbor, the UAE, but it offers stunning sands, turquoise waters, and beautiful buildings.

SOUTH KOREA

I promise, my crush on Korea isn't all about kimchi and K-pop. Seoul looks hip as hell, and it knows how to do streetwear. The more I delve into the fashion scene, the closer I am to booking my ticket.

AUSTRIA

It's not France, it's not Germany, it's all my *Sound of Music* alpine dreams come true!

FAROE ISLANDS

With jagged cliffs covered in electric-green moss, waterfalls that spill into the sea, and (wait for it) *puffins*, I struggle to believe that the Faroe Islands are real at all. If they are real, they must be inhabited entirely by fairies and jolly little Nordic trolls. There's only one way to find out, I guess.

NAMIBIA

If you think Montana has a big sky, think bigger. Namibia is famous for its jaw-dropping panoramas, vast silent deserts, and tall red dunes. My itinerary will include stargazing, sandboarding, and cheetah spotting.

EMERALD LAKE, BRITISH COLUMBIA, CANADA

So this one is very specific, but it's also the most beautiful thing I've never seen (but absolutely will one day). Tucked away in the snowcapped Canadian Rockies, flanked by lodgepole pines, Emerald Lake is the mind-bogglingly gorgeous blue-green jewel it promises to be. Apparently, most people just fawn over it or go for a paddle in a canoe, but I'm definitely swimming. I don't care how cold that glacier water is.

Pull Date: 12/8/2022

HOLD FOR:
7351
BAIRD CATHERIN

Placed on Hold Shelf: 11/30/2022
Title: Happily grey : stories, souvenirs, and ev
Item Number: 35192053713214

Thompson Lane Branch
HOLD SHELF SLIP

¡Salud!

(Of Course There's a) Mojito!

Drinking a mojito in Havana felt almost a little too touristy, but you better believe we did it anyway. Neither of us was sure where *our* relationship would go, but it was clear from day one that fresh mint, cane sugar, lime, and Havana Club white rum were destined to be together forever. I'll prove it to you.

YOU'LL NEED:

10 sprigs fresh mint

1½ teaspoons cane sugar

2 thin slices of fresh lime

Ice cubes

2 ounces white rum (sadly, you can't get Havana Club here)

1 ounce fresh lime juice

Club soda

STEPS:

1. Gently muddle mint, sugar, and lime slices in a tall 10-ounce glass that can take a joke. Don't get too crazy; chewing on the bigger mint bits after is the best part.
2. Fill the glass with 3 to 4 ice cubes.
3. Add rum and lime juice, stirring just a few times.
4. Top with club soda, give it one more stir, and *salud*!

CHAPTER 8
Always M

*The world isn't perfect, neither am I, and all of it really
is okay. Sometimes less than perfect is exactly right.*

Downtown Nashville is smaller than people think. On a Monday morning it's almost sleepy, an unassuming bunch of brown bricks, law offices, and back-alley barbecue pits packed with hickory wood and brisket. The bars open at 10 a.m., which is arguably a bit premature, but it's all middle-aged tourists learning the two-step and bargain shoppers looking to cash in on knockoff Tony Lamas. By noon things ramp up a bit: a party bus full of bachelorettes might roll by, hoisting their White Claws in the air and pretending they know all the words to "Jolene." A band of rowdy hockey fans might arrive to pregame for the Predators. In the afternoon there's a marked shift from Deadwood to Dollywood and when the sun goes down, it's Daytona Beach complete with bikini tops *and* boots.

Around 5 p.m. the neon comes blinking to life in green, burnt orange, and icy blue, hokey, big cartoonish guitars, and glowing cans of PBR. The bands on stage begin to play faster and louder. The cops place orange barricades below Fifth Avenue to block motorists out and invite pedestrians in. What was a normal, respectable city street becomes the

Honky Tonk Highway, a place where the good people of the Mid-South come to make questionable choices. The nice, middle-aged couple who was two-stepping at noon is either French kissing against the wall of the Margaritaville or headed for divorce. The bachelorette doesn't want to get married anymore. The hockey fans are shirtless. Nobody knows which way is up.

We don't finish with dinner until almost midnight, and since we're not in LA, there aren't a ton of places open for us to grab the twenty-dollar rococo nightcap we're looking for. Mad and I are with our friends, John and Tyler, who have been married a few years longer than we have and would probably be perfectly happy to head home, watch an episode of *The Office*, and stuff their faces into their pillows, which, honestly, doesn't sound too bad to me either. We stand on a street corner rifling through our options: a hipster place that seems to have a mandatory period of uncomfortable waiting in the vestibule or the hotel bar, where everything that should cost fifteen dollars costs forty.

"How about Broadway?" Tyler jokes.

Broadway.

John and Mad inhale sharply and in unison as we begin walking through the Gulch, a part of town that used to be a bit of a wasteland and is now the world capital of expensive parking and sushi. It's Friday night and we've all lived in Nashville long enough that we know better than to go downtown on the weekend. We're not too old for it—nobody is—but we are too sensible.

I wait for somebody to say no, for the Ubers to show up and the goodnight hugs, but we just keep walking. Before long, the hollow *clop* of our shoes is swallowed by steel guitar and we step into the mock sunrise of neon signs and spotlights.

The street is slammed when we slip past the barricade. I clutch Mad's hand so I don't get swept away by the current, which is mostly twenty-two-year-old women who smell like too much perfume and Jägermeister. Hopped up on Hank Williams, well whiskey, and pretty girls, a group of hockey fans suddenly become country music fans and jump onstage at the karaoke place. Thankfully, it's so loud that the pitchy notes are well hidden in the sonic tangle of banjo, screaming, and dueling pianos. A drunk lady pushes a sensible-looking man in the chest outside Ernest Tubb Record Shop, but the cops who are waiting nearby decide she's not sober enough to do any damage. With a wide smile on her face, Tyler follows a crew of wannabe cowboys from New England toward the waterfront on a mission: find a bar, get a drink, get out *quick*. We do our best to keep up without bumping anyone the wrong way.

After my divorce, when a pal would visit or the right mood would strike, I'd find myself at a honky-tonk. I'd made good friends. We were almost all single creatives in our twenties and dead broke. Broadway opened its arms to us with two-dollar beers, free bluegrass, and no dress code. We used to dance with the little old rockabillies at Robert's Western World, sing along to George Jones covers, grab cheap burgers at 11 p.m., and make a few (mostly harmless) mistakes: kiss a stranger, dance on a stage, make sloppy new best friends with people in town for a convention. I haven't done anything like that in a long time; I'm married now and trying to eat plant based. The fun has more or less been snuffed out, or at the very least heavily sedated.

"We used to go there every Friday and sit at the back of the bar," I remember out loud.

Mad peers inside Robert's. It's packed when we pass by, but I can still see a few little old guys in ranchwear spinning tourists on the dance floor. I can smell the damn-good hamburgers cooking on the grill.

We settle in at a smaller bar where they've got room for us. It might be Second Fiddle, but I never stopped to look at the sign. The band is taking their break, so the crowd has spilled onto the street to take Instagram photos and smoke American Spirits. I spot a row of stools at the bar and grab them, ordering gin and tonics for Mad and I. Tyler and John watch wide-eyed as a redheaded couple stumble onto the empty dance floor to do nothing but make out to "Friends in Low Places" played through the crackly old speakers.

Mad kisses me on the head and smiles. "We should do this more often."

We probably should. I steam my jeans more often than I let loose.

Hydrated and satiated, the band starts up again, the crowd returns from their Frito pies and fistfights. In the corner of the room, a bride-to-be yells, "I f****** love you, Nashville!" then takes a double shot of something murky, slamming the glass down to an eruption of cheers and camera flashes. A hansom cab rolls past the front window and the big dappled grey horse with feet the size of dinner plates gives me a knowing look, straight in the eye, and the night begins to feel like an impossible collaboration between Luke Bryan and Lewis Carroll. I take a long sip of my drink and relax into the chaos.

"Mad!" I shout over "The Devil Went Down to Georgia." "Let's get tattoos!"

He looks at me and scrunches his eyebrows, giving me a good once-over and trying to decide if I'm sober. I am.

"You guys are crazy." Tyler laughs, shaking her head. She and John are always up for a drink after dinner, but they draw the line at group body modification.

We turn off Broadway and away from the well-oiled masses to catch a few breaths of fresh air. Mad found a place open late that has 4.8 stars on Yelp and we all agree that it looks (kind of) clean in the pictures. Our trust in Yelp runs deep, but I wonder if we should be going to it for tattoo guidance the way we do for taco guidance. The city air gets crisper as we walk and I pull my jacket tight around my shoulders, crossing my arms over my chest, taking a second to look down at my last tattoo, *"be."* on my left wrist, which took months of preparing and soul-searching and rigorous font auditioning to decide on. Tonight, I'll be lucky if I don't end up with a Tasmanian devil on the side of my neck.

After a long uphill climb, we arrive at the shop, which is decidedly less clean in person but still clean enough. John holds the door open and the four of us file into a poorly lit, shallow-ceilinged room with splotches of water damage and walls decorated like my childhood sticker book. There is a patch of wall with Chinese characters, another patch with roses, and a large section I can only describe as "skulls, spiders, and miscellaneous satanic iconography." A man behind the counter, who is grumpy and bald, grunts at us but doesn't say hello. His gruffness is a relief. I'd never trust a bubbly tattoo artist working the graveyard shift.

Mad walks over to the wall and looks at the stars, desperate to find meaning in something before he slaps it on his body. I consider the anchors and Polynesian-looking strings of whitecaps. We're not exactly seafaring people, but nobody's mad at the ocean and I've always loved a nautical-style moment. John threatens to get a giant skateboarding Bart Simpson on his scapula. Tyler threatens to get a Homer on her lower back. I laugh a deep, rib-stretching laugh and promise to remember it all: the smell of Clorox and ink, the too-bright lighting, and the good, good people.

The man at the counter shifts and begins to grumble, alerting us to the fact that we've nearly outstayed our welcome. "Shit or get off the pot, lassie," he seems to say with just his eyebrows.

"What about 'always m'?" I ask.

Both of our names begin with *M*, and we've been married about a year, so maybe it can be an anniversary thing? Either that or it can be the title of a god-awful YA series.

Mad sits with it for a few seconds and nods. "I love it."

"Really?" I ask, wishing that he was up for adventure a little less of the time.

"Yep. Let's do it!"

I pull my sleeve up, find a spot below my elbow, and walk up to the speckled Formica counter like I'm about to order a milkshake and curly fries, wishing I looked and felt less like Sandra Dee.

"Hi." I smile at the crusty, shiny-headed giant. "We're ready now. Can you help us?"

He says nothing to me. He slaps on a pair of latex gloves and yells, "Marrrrk!"

Another bald gentleman pops out of a back room to join us, but he looks more like he works on computers than Harleys. I decide that one can be Mad's guy.

"What are y'all thinking?" he asks.

Normally in a situation like ours, a person might draw the design out first, experiment with the lettering, discuss whether the *M* should be in quotes or freestanding. We do none of those things. In what feels like seconds, Mad and I are seated in the vinyl dentist-office chairs and the tattoo artists are revving up their needles. All we've decided is that the font should be something "script-ish."

The scary man works on my arm while the nerdy one works on Mad, which I realize is fundamentally problematic if our sort-of-anniversary tattoos are going to look anything alike. It's too late to turn back though. The needle is boring its way into my skin and I'm just trying not to look down. Tyler says, "Okay, guys, we're doing it," and John, who is the kindest, sweetest soul, assures us that it's all going to turn out great. For reasons that will remain mysterious, I'm totally at ease. A few feet away, Mad tries to smile through the burn and wrinkles his nose.

"It's okay." I don't know why I say it or who I'm telling. Maybe Mad, who is stretched out on his chair like it's a pool lounge and clearly doesn't need the encouragement. Maybe Tyler, who can't believe we're actually going through with it. Maybe I'm just telling myself. It's abundantly clear that these tattoos are not going to be great art pieces. We'll be lucky if we aren't permanently branded with Comic Sans or Looney Tunes characters, but it's okay. It really is. Not every mistake becomes a regret. I'll remember this night, the joy of it, the color in John's cheeks, the crispness of the air, forever.

There are a few more minutes of buzzing and stinging but then the needles doze off, the men roll their wheelie chairs away from us, and we all take in the artisanship.

"Look at that," Mad says, peering down at my arm.

My skin is so puffy all I can see is a worm-shaped blue-black line. All I can hope is that it'll say what it's supposed to when the swelling goes down. I look over at Mad's arm. It's in even worse shape than mine. The men slather Vaseline on our arms, cover them in plastic wrap, and help us stand up on our adrenaline-shocked legs. Mad swipes his credit card and we each get a plastic bag with a tube of cream, a business card, and a coupon for 10 percent off our next piercing. Altogether, our tattoos cost eighty dollars. They aren't worth a penny more.

"You guys next?" the cranky guy says to John and Tyler. Their eyes get big, and they rush for the door. I don't think I'll ever stop laughing.

By morning, the thrill and swelling have both subsided. I wake up with throbbing temples and blistered toes, pulling my arm out from under the duvet to examine my skin, which is less pink than I expected. The blue-black ink, though still slightly risen, is shockingly legible. Mad's arm falls over my body and I retreat into the pillow, happy for a few more minutes to just be. In a perfect world, I might have gone for a font that looked a little bit less like it belonged on a Hobby Lobby wall hanging, but the world isn't perfect, neither am I, and all of it really is okay. Sometimes less than perfect is exactly right.

Keep SAKES

Always *M*

When I listen to "Born to Be Wild" by Steppenwolf, I feel nothing. I mean, I don't hate rolling down the window and screaming that chorus, but I'm not relating to it, or James Dean or Lori Petty in *Point Break* or *Catwoman*, on any deep, personal level. I have a profound appreciation for the rebels of the world, but despite a love of leather moto jackets, I cannot count myself among them. Somebody needs to write a song called "Born to Be Next to a Fireplace with a Glass of Sauvignon Blanc."

I'm (mostly) happy to report, though, that being with Mad has emboldened me slightly. I take more risks and let my hair down with a little less prodding. I feel lighter, less weighed down by doubts, decisions, and the desire to color within the lines. Apparently, sometimes I get love tattoos in the middle of the night with no forethought whatsoever. The world just isn't as scary when you know somebody loves you. At least not in the moment.

"always m" is equal parts victory and failure. I did something impulsive (win), but it's tattooed on my body forever (whoops!). Even though it isn't the world's most refined example of body art, I've grown fond of my wobbly forearm tribute to wild nights, good friends, and true love. And it can't be a mistake if I like it, right?

My Favorite Mistakes

Sometimes something is so bad, it's good, especially with fashion. When I love something, I love it, and no matter how many platform-shoe interventions my team stages for me, I just won't stop. Here are some wrongs that feel so, so right:

—Stupid-Big Sleeves
—Vintage Without a Modern Twist
—Adult Pigtails
—Everything Oversized
—Trend Overload
—Accessory Overload
—Prints on Prints on Prints on Prints
—Big Ol' Chunky Shoes

Skydiving
for Perfectionists

I spent the first thirtyish years of my life trying to be a flawless human being, which at the time seemed like a reasonable goal. Growing up I didn't want to be good at one sport—I wanted to be good at all of them. I did basketball and cross-country and volleyball and tumbling and cheerleading and fast-pitch softball (we won state!). It wasn't good enough to excel at all the sports. I had to excel at school, too, and piano and church (I didn't get the memo, but they don't give out awards in Sunday school). In other words, I was buckets of fun and they would have kicked me out of the Little Rascals on the first day.

Aside from the fact that my perfectionism was totally unrealistic, it was also unhealthy. I did mostly what I knew I was good at, I constantly criticized my body, and I missed out on a whole lot of growth. I had to put some real emotional muscle into becoming okay with being just okay. At first, opening myself up to the possibility of failure felt like skydiving, and though I can't say that I celebrate when a brand doesn't call to work with me again or I notice a new wrinkle on my forehead or I get a bad tattoo, I don't panic either. Recovering perfectionism, let's get average!

COOK WITHOUT A RECIPE

Brace yourself for some salty cookies, friend! Seriously, though, cooking guided only by instinct (and hope!) is a great reminder that not everything needs to be done by the book. Madison Lee does this All. The. Time. and has a total blast doing it. Sometimes the culinary Imagineering turns out wonderfully, and other times it's a flop. Thankfully, the world doesn't end if the chicken is bland.

COVER UP YOUR MIRROR

Because I love my outfits, this one hurts bad. I can't pose or preen or change bags ten times. I just concentrate on feeling good instead of looking good. Of course, I cheat whenever I'm in the Whole Foods bathroom, but it turns out that when I feel great, it shows.

DO KARAOKE (UNLESS YOU'RE AMAZING AT KARAOKE)

There are certain things in life that are most perfect when they are not perfect at all. Karaoke is one of those things. It has more to do with your balls than your pipes and nothing brings the house down like a spectacular fail with *feeling*. I highly recommend Shania.

STREAM-OF-CONSCIOUSNESS JOURNALING

Go! Write! Now! Punctuation optional! No outlines allowed! In journaling, nothing is wrong; you can use any "two/to/too" you want.

SHOW UP LATE

Don't make a habit of it, but you'll notice that to regular folk, the gulf between 9 a.m. and 9:05 a.m. is not as wide as you may think.

FOCUS ON GRATITUDE

Channel all that "big achiever" mojo into something different. When I shift my focus from being the most successful to being the most grateful, mistakes matter less, and people matter more.

The Best Things on Lower Broadway

Talk to a local about Lower Broad and they'll just shake their head, but chances are you'll run into each other around midnight between The Stage and Jack's Bar-B-Que. Playing too loud since the 1930s, Nashville's entertainment district is like nothing else—wild, welcoming, a little tipsy, and a lot of fun. It's impossible to get off the Honky Tonk Highway without a good story and a gnarly hangover. If you don't know where to begin your Broadway journey, start here:

THE RECESSION SPECIAL AT ROBERT'S

Not only is Robert's—the rarely disputed king of bars on Broadway—a vibe in and of itself and my personal favorite place to hang downtown, it has one of the best meals in the city. For six bucks you get a fried bologna sandwich, a bag of chips, a PBR, and a Moon Pie for dessert. Don't sleep on their burger either.

THE BAND AT LAYLA'S

In recent years Broadway has gone more bro country than hillbilly, but Layla's is still hanging on to the good old stuff. Stop here for bluegrass, newgrass, Americana, and rockabilly.

NOSEBLEEDS AT THE NASHVILLE PREDATORS

The person who decided to plunk down an NHL hockey team in the middle of a bunch of cowboys was a mad genius. It turns out, hockey fans and honky-tonkers are made of the same rowdy stuff. It doesn't matter where you sit, the energy is everywhere. Cheer for the home team and head out with your new best friends after (hockey fans are super friendly).

Lovers, fighters, fiddlers, college kids, cowboys . . . we've got all of it.

LITERALLY *ANYONE* PLAYING AT THE RYMAN

The Mother Church! Motörhead could play the Ryman and they'd sound like a chorale of baby angels. No visit to Nashville is complete without sitting in the pews and taking in a show. Local music highly recommended.

LEG QUARTER AND "GET IT GIRL" GREENS
AT PRINCE'S HOT CHICKEN

Nashville hot chicken may be popping up everywhere, but nowhere is better than Prince's. Warning: Crunchy fried chicken covered in five-alarm fire is no joke. Start with the mild and work your way up.

PRINTER'S ALLEY

If you were looking for a drink during prohibition, there's a good chance you'd find one in Printer's Alley. Once home to Nashville's publishing industry, then home to jazz, brown-bagged booze, and wise guys, Printer's Alley has retained every ounce of its irresistible seedy charm. Take a stroll down this literal memory lane between Third and Fourth avenues and hit Bourbon Street Blues and Boogie Bar for a NOLA-style hurricane.

THE PEOPLE

After dark, Lower Broadway has some of the best people-watching on planet Earth. Lovers, fighters, fiddlers, college kids, cowboys . . . we've got all of it.

CHAPTER 9
Scars

A scar tells a story of healing, not pain.

The incision runs across my pelvis, deep below my hip bones and just above the place where my legs split from the center of me. I couldn't feel it when it happened—the severing of skin, the shock of my insides meeting the outside for the first time—but I feel all of it now. Baby Navy is here. She's safe, she's perfect, and she made it to the other side with pink cheeks and powerful lungs. But I'm not sure I did.

My love for her is complete and constant. It started the moment she entered this world and stopped time with a perfect first scream, and it will go on forever. I love her when she practices nursing in her sleep, when her cry is a soft whinny at 3 a.m., and when, for reasons only God understands, her lips curl up into a totally elated, totally toothless smile. I'm filled with joy when the house is loud and cooing and alive, but when the sky gets dark and everything goes quiet, there's nothing but grief. Nobody is gone, but still, I'm grieving.

Mad is in bed, shirt off, eyes closed, chin covered in a week's worth of beard that maybe he'll get to or maybe he won't. We've been parents for six days. He swaddled Navy all by himself in one of the printed muslin blankets I agonized over choosing but now can hardly tell

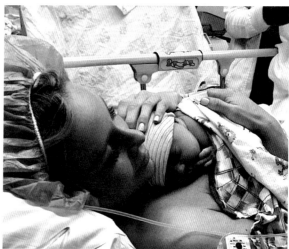
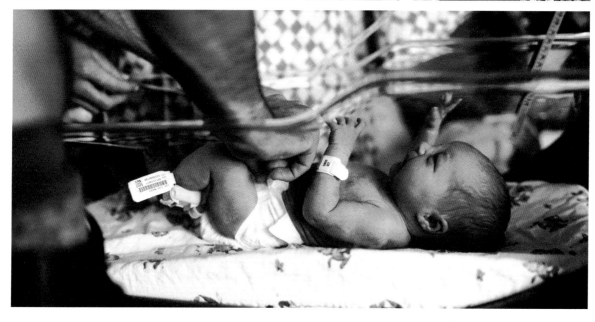

apart from the others. I watched him from the bathroom, tenderly tucking her arms next to her sides, folding the extra fabric underneath her bottom. He kissed the tiny wisps of hair on her head, placed her in the bassinet next to the bed, and fell into REM sleep in a nanosecond. The very next nanosecond, Navy's arms are batting the dust hanging in the afternoon light.

I walk over to the bassinet and smile at her. She's the size of a turkey leg and as strong as an ox. Slowly, I wrap her again and kiss her again and take a drink of her through my nose—she smells like hospital bracelet and milk. Her lips are little red minnows that swim in place under her nose and she doesn't really have eyebrows yet. She takes up virtually no space in the world but has managed to change it completely. I pause to count her eyelashes and the wrinkles on her knuckles. Less than a week into motherhood, I feel like I've known my baby for a hundred lifetimes, but I'm a stranger to myself.

Slowly, I lower my own body into our unmade, musty bed, which looked clean and modern before we left for the hospital but now looks like it belongs in a Berlin youth hostel. Patches of blood and breast milk make a map of the last twenty-four hours on the sheets, every unsuccessful attempt to get comfortable marked with its own stain and smell. All I do is try to get comfortable—in my bed, in my skin, in my spirit.

There are little piles of "trying" everywhere: the nursing bras I tried before I realized there was no point in bras at all, the silver cups that keep my nipples from cracking (when I can actually find both of them), the instructions to the sound machine that we tried that was supposed to remind her of the womb but reminded us more of *The Tell-Tale Heart*. There's the half bowl of chili on the bedstand that I tried to eat but couldn't because none of my internal organs have decided where they'd like to settle down just yet. There are the invisible things that take up space too. Shock, mourning, shame, confusion, and fear—they shrink the room into a closet. Nothing but the love feels right.

I was supposed to have a natural birth. She wasn't supposed to have meconium in her mouth. I was supposed to breastfeed the hour after she was born and it was supposed to go easily. I was supposed to feel like a warrior. Mad snuffles from the middle of a dream and Navy snuffles after him.

The weight of my body shifts from my ankles to the mattress, and I try to revel in something while I rest, the simple joy of lying on my back again or the taste of water. Instead, I notice a cobweb I can't reach fluttering against the white of the ceiling. Suddenly, I'm overcome. I remember everything.

The hospital gown is soaking wet and I'm shivering. My teeth are chattering from the Pitocin, the contractions, and the worry. Mad's hand is on mine. He's been quiet most of the time and it's exactly what I need from him. I can't think or speak or process when the cramps come barking up my side. I've been in labor for almost twenty hours, but my body isn't listening to me—the body I spent months preparing for this, and years before that, exercising and feeding it properly so that it would be prepared for anything. The body that can run an eight-minute mile before morning coffee can't seem to perform the most essential and basic task in its repertoire. It isn't keeping Navy safe anymore. Her heart rate is abnormal. I'm bleeding and we don't know why. I waddle around the birthing suite, bracing myself on the prefab hospital furniture and squatting beside the bed, breathing the way our doula says will relax me. It doesn't though. The nurse comes bounding in to check on me. She's a ball of cheerful with lilac scrubs and dimples. Gently, she helps me haul my body up onto the bed and places my feet in the stirrups, one after the other. I swear, I feel it at the top of my skull when she pokes at my cervix.

"You're still at three centimeters," she says, and I watch a little ribbon of worry cross her forehead.

She studies the foothills of activity on the screen and adjusts the stretchy transducer belts around my middle, one pastel blue and the other pastel pink. The fetal monitor releases a slow *ding-dong* like the doorbell of a fancy house and everything changes. The nurse isn't cheerful anymore. Her dimples are gone. Hurriedly, she shoves me onto my side.

"Her heart rate dropped below seventy."

Navy's pulse had been dipping for the last ten hours, but it always comes back up. It doesn't this time.

"I'm going to get the doctor. It's time." Her voice is the way they've trained it to be, unpanicked but grave. Within seconds, there are ten people in the room.

Mad's eyes triple in size and in one swoop, I rake the jewelry from my limbs and drop it onto his lap. I'm in nurse mode now, ready to do what's necessary, casting away the almost ten-month-old hopes of the dreamy birth in the giant inflatable tub. I focus on my daughter's birth like a professional, not a patient. I leave my body completely.

The lights are so hot and so white in the OR that the faces of the people working on my body are just flesh-colored orbs. Mad is next to me now in his gown, hiding with me behind the big blue barrier and making sure I keep my arms in a giant *T*.

"It's okay," I tell him.

I don't need to tell myself because I'm in crisis mode. I've been trained for this. I go back to the dozen or so c-sections I watched in nursing school. *It's all routine.*

The anesthesiologist comes in to give me the spinal block. I got an epidural twelve hours ago, but it only worked on one side of my body. I feel an icy, slick alcohol pad slipping over the bumps of my spine and then nothing else. My brain works independently from the rest of me and I go over the steps as they happen:

First, they'll do the initial incision.

Next, they'll cut through the fat and separate your muscles.

If they need to move your bladder and your intestines, they will.

They just did. Did you feel that?

The smell? Nothing to worry about. They're cauterizing the blood vessels. The sound? That's suctioning, they're removing amniotic fluid.

There's going to be pressure, the baby's head and shoulders are coming.

She's out! There's a little meconium. The NICU team will take her over to the warmer and suction her.

There she is. You have a daughter.

Time stands unmoving and I hear my breath. I hear her cry. I feel the lights on my face. I feel the warmth of a new, strange, desperate, forever love.

"You did it!" Mad mumbles to me from under his mask, tears rolling down his cheeks and onto mine. He kisses me and brushes my hair with his fingers through the plastic covering on my head. I'm allowed to release my arms from the muscle-melting crucifix pose I've been holding for the past twenty minutes. After a full NICU assessment, the nurse places Navy on my chest and I get lost in holding her, watching her blink, taking in the miracle of motherhood.

For three beautiful days, I nurse and change diapers and behold her, but then we go home. The crisis is over. When we walk through the door, I return to the body that failed me.

I bury my head in the pillow as I revisit every frame, simultaneously trying to remember and forget the birth of my daughter *and* of my new self. Sadness rumbles through me in big, heavy, wetter-than-wet tears. Then shame comes. I feel messy and disgusted with myself. I didn't show up for my own baby. I didn't give her the right start. All she needed me to do

was exactly what my body was designed to do, and I couldn't. I hold back another deep sob, trying to dodge the pain in my abdomen and the pain in my boobs, which are leaking and the size of conventional watermelons. Mad wraps his arms around me, not understanding and not able to understand, clamoring to be in it with me. He's only seen me cry a few times before and never like this. I'm completely undone.

Navy roars back to consciousness with a ravenous, high-pitched scream. Because it's easier, because I'm good in crisis mode, I leave my body once again:

First, you feed the baby.

Then, you burp her.

Next, you put her in a new diaper.

It goes on and on and I wonder if I'll ever forgive myself, find myself, or love myself again.

I do, though, because bodies are wise and because time is a good teacher, and because, like Navy, I'm brand-new here. As she wakes up to her world, I wake up to mine. It is slow and it is painful; it is joyful and it goes too fast; it defies logic and it makes perfect sense. Over time the body that felt strange and empty fills up with light and warmth. It becomes home, the safest, most sacred place in the world.

Months go by. My boobs shrink back down to a smaller, somewhat more manageable size, like organic cantaloupe, maybe. My stomach doesn't sting anymore when I laugh, and slowly, as I return to myself, I *do* laugh, often. The incision that I hated fades into a long whiteish seam that I can hide away neatly in my underwear. I explore my new world the way the baby explores hers. It isn't what I know, but I remember the joy in not knowing and delight in the unearthing of motherhood.

Navy James's eyes grow into big, blue, curious skies in the middle of her face. She makes "ba, ba, ba" sounds and likes to look at herself in the mirror. She likes books we don't expect about dinosaurs and shapes, and foods we don't expect like tomatoes. She walks early, around eleven months, pulling up on the furniture and on the dogs, opening drawers and doors and never tiring of the things and people and feelings around her. Everything she discovers, I discover again with her: the feeling of grass on the soles of my feet, the taste of ripe banana, butterfly kisses just like the ones my dad used to give me, and endlessly hilarious, magically iridescent, perfectly poppable bubbles! Everything that she loves, I love too. Including myself.

My body nurtured her body. I was her home, her fortress, her safe place. I still am. My

job was to hold her, and I held her tight, ignoring the Pitocin and the muscle spasms, refusing to go numb when the medicine asked, unrelenting until the moment she was christened in the cool, sterile air. It wasn't what we planned, but it was natural, guided entirely by my body's instinct to love, protect, and keep her.

When she reaches for my face, I don't just forgive my body—I praise it. When she laughs at the way we look in the mirror together, I don't just smile at the reflection—I revel in it. When I dry bathwater from the long, jagged scar she left me with, I don't just feel love—I feel astounding, endless, life-giving gratitude. I still feel messy, but I *am* messy. I am messy and I am beautiful. I follow the raised flesh with my fingers, staring down at the wonderful sheen of new skin, in awe. A scar tells a story of healing, not pain.

Navy turns one in June 2020 and in so many ways, so do I. We throw her a party with rose-gold balloons and as many black-and-white photos of her first year as Costco would let us print. She gets an art easel for her new playroom with finger paints and dot markers and big sticks of chalk. She spends her day giggling and creating, covered in primary colors and delighted. I gift myself something, too, a new portrait that tells a messy, beautiful, wonderful story of *our* birth.

Keep SAKES

Scars

I didn't recognize myself. I felt like a failure. I'd lost a sense of home in my own body. I never talked about it. We need to talk about it.

Navy's birth was traumatic. Sometime between the twentieth and twenty-fourth hours of laboring, I abandoned the body that I felt had abandoned me. When I needed and wanted to come back to myself, I couldn't find the way. Everything was different. *I* was different. My boobs were the size of small moons and I didn't trust myself. My abdomen was stapled shut and the rest of me was shut down. While my whole world celebrated, I grieved. Nothing went the way I wanted it to. Motherhood felt more like an end than a beginning. But sometimes, that's the way beginnings work.

In small, shuffling steps to the bathroom, great big secret tears, and sleeplessness, I learned grace. I forgave myself, not for failing to meet my expectations but for setting them in the first place. I learned to love the soft silvery stripes on my skin, the sweetness of breast milk on my clothes, the long pink incision between my hips, the border my Navy crossed to meet me here. When I thought motherhood was breaking me, it was busy healing me, teaching me, and welcoming me.

I forgave myself, not for failing to meet my expectations but for setting them in the first place.

Baby Your Belly

As a child, I guessed I would have *at least* ten babies. Sticking a couch cushion under my shirt and waddling around like I'd slipped a disc, I loved imagining what I would look like and how I would feel on the precipice of motherhood. It turns out, I would feel like a blue whale with sciatica and an aversion to beets. I hoped for a gargantuan belly, and I got one. Taking care of it was no small task, but these things made a big difference.

BELLY BAND

Support was key for relieving my achy lower back in the third trimester and for bracing my abdomen after the c-section. I wore it anytime I was on my feet.

PREGNANCY PILLOW

Not being able to get comfortable in bed can take even the most luminous expectant mother to a real dark place. A pregnancy pillow (or small village of regular pillows) can make the mandatory side sleeping a little more tolerable.

EXERCISE

I was so lucky to be able to exercise throughout my pregnancy. It helped me stay sane and kept me strong enough to support my super bump. Postpartum, after my doctor gave me the okay, I started a gentle daily core workout at home. Tummy time for everyone!

RED RASPBERRY LEAF TEA

It's tasty *and* it tones your uterus. The week after my c-section, I looked five months pregnant and started RRLT drinking daily (yes, it's caffeine-free), hoping it would help me regain my core. It could have been the sleep deprivation, but over time I noticed pretty impressive results.

LOTS OF CREAM

The tiny glass canisters of stretch-mark cream you can barely fit your index finger into might seem cute in the beginning, but when you really start to grow, you'll need a vat of it. I needed so much of it, I ended up developing my own damn product! If you find something you like, look out for multipacks or BOGO deals.

A NEW MINDSET

Our bellies are supposed to look different and feel different, both during and after pregnancy. Skin stretches, muscles slacken, bodies shift, priorities change, but beauty, purpose, and wonder remain. Your post-baby body is not just "how it is"—it's exactly as it should be.

Your post-baby body is not just "how it is" —it's exactly as it should be.

The Itty-Bitty Nitty-Gritty

Before Navy got here, I assumed I had more than cursory knowledge concerning infant care. I worked (briefly, but still) in a NICU and I spent my childhood devotedly raising more than a dozen plastic dolls. Once, before a family road trip to Eureka Springs, Arkansas, my dad refused to let me take the whole brood with me *unless* I could name them all. He stood wide-eyed (and probably regretful) as I did. Even though I was a model parent at just nine years old (word on the Cabbage Patch is that baby Sally got into Yale and baby Poppy is a Broadway actress), there are things about having my own human baby that I was not prepared for, things that none of our parent friends were bold enough to tell us. Today, I'm feeling bold.

BREASTFEEDING IS *NOT* NATURAL

I mean, it is . . . but it's very possible that it won't feel that way. When your boobs triple in size and develop strange, nippley spider senses, you might feel straight-up alarmed. I sure did! Call in a lactation consultant, ask friends for help, and remember, it's okay if it doesn't work for you. Fed is best. Sure, women have been doing it for thousands of years, but we all start from day one. Go easy on yourself.

SWADDLING IS A HIGHER ART FORM

Unless you work at a Chipotle or have a raging origami habit, you might not hit the ground running with the whole swaddle thing. There's nothing wrong with you; babies are expert wigglers and those reflexes are real. Practice makes perfect (but sleep sacks can help too).

*I was a hungry pregnant lady,
but I was a ravenous nursing lady.*

CLUSTER FEEDING IS A THING

Sometimes the baby eats every two to three hours, but early on and during growth spurts, little one might have a much bigger appetite. Cluster feeding is characterized by short, frequent nursing sessions over the course of a few hours, and for us, it normally happened in the evening. Find a comfortable spot, sign in to Netflix, and lean in.

BABY AND MAMA WILL EAT ALL DAY

I was a hungry pregnant lady, but I was a ravenous nursing lady. When your body is making milk and taking names, life is a full-on snack attack. The solution is easy. Listen to your body and eat.

THE BABY? YOU MIGHT NOT LIKE HER

You'll probably *love* the baby, but really, you might not like her. Bonding can take time. At 2 a.m., when you haven't gotten a stretch of sleep longer than forty minutes and there's a small rosy-cheeked tyrant yelling at you, don't be surprised if you consider yelling back. Call in your partner, a family member, a postpartum doula. It's okay to need a little space and it's also okay to talk to your doctor if you feel like you need extra support.

YOU DON'T WANT TO HAVE SEX

Fair enough, sister! Now you know what all that rolling around leads to! Seriously though, you're depleted, your hormones are crazy, your boobs are leaky, and you haven't brushed your hair in six weeks. When the doctor gives you the okay, it's totally fine to make it a "no way" until you feel ready.

BABY MONITOR IN, IPHONE OUT

The baby will sleep, and then you'll stare at the baby sleeping. Your eyes will start to hurt. *Have you really been watching the baby sleep for a full hour?!* Yes, you have. There's a new screen in your life and you should also try not to lose yourself in this one. Rest. Take a hot shower. Eat more snacks. Trust me, the baby will be up soon.

Don't use the purple ones—they stain!

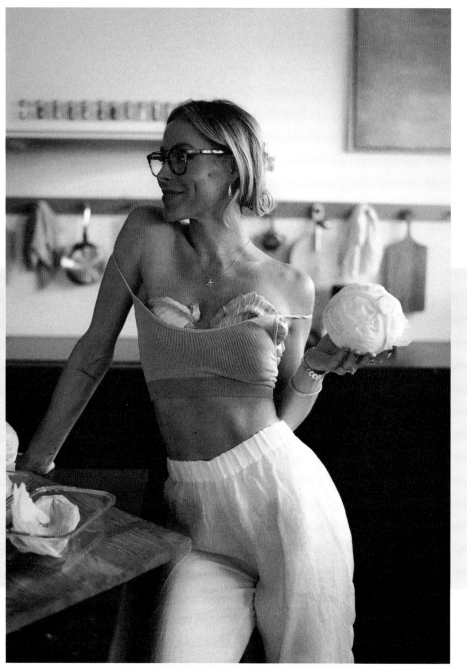

The Cabbage Bra

I have a very big heart and very small breasts. It's how I've always been; it's how I always will be. Two days after little baby Navy was born, I woke up with a searing pain in my chest only to discover that my boobs had quintupled in size overnight. It was not pretty. Those things were as heavy as kettlebells. I tried icing them and heating them. I tried pumping and praying, but what helped me more than anything else with engorgement was a beloved, oft-dismissed, totally unbe-leaf-able trick called the Cabbage Bra. Let's get you some relief and a sweet vegan bikini!

YOU'LL NEED:

1 cabbage

1 wireless bra

An open mind

STEPS:

1. Separate, clean, and dry several green cabbage leaves. Don't use the purple ones—they stain!

2. Chill the leaves in the refrigerator (or the freezer if you're a true thrill seeker) for thirty minutes to one hour.

3. Line the cups of a comfortable wireless bra with a few chilled leaves, enough to cover each breast completely.

4. Carefully put the bra on and relax until the leaves get warm or you get tired of smelling like sauerkraut.

5. Repeat as needed.

CHAPTER 10

Messy Bun

*What happens when documenting life
becomes more important than living it?*

I am known best for a picture of the back of my head.

Under a shadowy, overcast sky, I'm walking away from the camera wearing a green varsity jacket covered in giant stars. My hair is long and swept up into the most perfectly imperfect messy bun and I'm looking back, just slightly. This image becomes my greatest hit, an unexpected, totally accidental magnum opus.

In 2016, I make my mark on the internet with a hairdo, the messy bun. It gets thousands of likes on Instagram and Pinterest, and even though becoming a hair icon was never my intention, it gets the ball rolling. People share pictures of *their* messy buns, make messy bun video tutorials, and thank me profusely for leading them to cockeyed updo victory. It's just a picture of hair, of hair that could belong to anyone, but for some reason, some mysterious internet chain reaction, it defines me. I am messy bun. Messy bun is me. Of all the things I thought I'd be remembered for, my buns are not one of them. Not those buns anyway.

Today is busy, like all days are at *Happily Grey*. Bun-mania 2016 is a lingering memory but in the years since then, demand for content has ramped up, quintupled, not just for me but for everyone. I've never been able to stay on top of it all. I scroll back and revisit the bun often, trying to isolate the moment when everything changed, when I transformed from a person into a personality. Because I can't resist, I peek down at the comments.

"Take off your sunglasses!" one follower writes.

"How come you never show us your face?!" barks another.

"RAY-BANS. Brand New. 90 percent off DM for details," adds one more, using me as a billboard until the inevitable deletion.

Blogging barely exists anymore. It might as well be a hard copy of the daily paper. It's far too much work for people to go to a website, shuffle through their digital to-do lists, and read a post longer than two thousand characters. The blog is still there, but it doesn't move fast enough or flash enough to catch anyone's attention. You're nowhere if you're not on Instagram (and TikTok and YouTube and all the other places), so that's where I spend most of my time. The survival of the brand depends on it. A small team and I spend the days trying to fulfill the silent ultimatum for more: more new content, more pictures, more stories, more advertisements. We sit in an open-concept office warding off tension headaches with glasses that fight against the blue tint and reckon with the truth of what we do. These days, if you're not giving all of yourself, you're not giving enough. You can tell people all day long to set healthy boundaries, just as long as you don't have any yourself.

When I started *Happily Grey*, it was all about fashion. That's what I wanted it to be. The idea that I would become yet another size-small, blonde-haired, upper-middle-class guru sharing her wisdom with the world, one vanity project after another, *made me cringe*. It still does. I stepped onto social media platforms like I was walking a plank. I wanted a level of privacy. I wanted space for myself. That's why I took pictures of the back of my head. That's why the sunglasses were on. That's why I refuse to tell anybody how they should be living their life. I just tell them how to dress while they're doing it. It isn't enough though. People want to know how many calories I eat in a day and if I've had Botox done. If I did have the Botox done, where did I do it? What are my feelings on all of it? Why did I get divorced? Was it hard to get pregnant? Did I have a natural birth? Do we have a nanny for Navy? Why did I get vaccinated? Do I have an eating disorder? Did I have an eating disorder? How do I *really* feel?

I spend the first part of my morning in the office editing campaigns and stressing about deadlines and then another hour replying to comments and DMs, but then I head off to a shoot, passing the account off to my assistant who can answer most questions for me.

"Sorry," I tell her. "I know it's a pain, but I want people to know that they matter."

She smiles and laughs. "It's no big deal, Mary. It's mostly just emojis."

I wish that were less true. I grab my bag and watch her crack her knuckles, preparing to post kissy-face, kissy-face, kissy-face, triple heart, "*thanks, girl*" three thousand times in a row.

We're a small team of nine, and though we have titles, we share responsibilities. We all do trash runs and break down boxes. We all strategize and brainstorm. There are a lot of hats to wear, but thankfully we are all hat people. We work together and we work hard. That's what small business is.

Our photographer, Jessica, is downstairs waiting for me. We've known each other for years; she knows me and the brand inside and out. We're shooting a campaign for a designer highlighting his upcoming fall collection. It's still a hundred degrees in Nashville, but that's okay—we'll shoot now, share the assets with the brand, and then post them when the weather drops below seventy-five. I put on a cable-knit sweater and tall, black riding boots even though the leaves are electric green and the sun is in the middle of the sky. I grab one coffee from the place in the lobby to drink and another coffee just to take photos of. The barista spends extra time on the show coffee, making a heart in the foam, asking me to tag them when he passes it across the bar. Oh, and tag the people who made the mug too. And the roaster, who's based out of Chicago. Tag Chicago too.

Jess fiddles with her lenses while I place the show coffee on a patio table outside and stand over it, trying to get the light just right on my phone, knowing that it doesn't matter, knowing that I'll put it through some filter anyway and that it'll look more like a moody crème brulée in the end. The coffee I bought to drink gets cold while I find the right angle on the other one.

"Mary," she calls. "Let's grab a few where you're moving."

I abandon what's left of my drink and join her on the sidewalk in front of a red-brick facade.

"Just walk," she says.

"Where to?" I ask.

"Doesn't matter," she shrugs.

And it doesn't matter. I march back and forth in front of my building acting like I'm on my way somewhere important when really, I'm just playing pretend. I go on to spend hours styling the looks, scouting the locations, putting together a creative brief for the team. I bring four looks with me and change in the car like a teenager on the way to her after-school job at Dairy Queen. The process isn't always pretty, but the pictures are and that's what people care about. They want content, stories, how-tos, and little glimpses of life. They want more. But the more people want of me, the less they get. They get a product I never even meant to create, neatly packaged for popular consumption.

Do we have enough now? I ask myself.

No.

I'm breathing heavily. It's August and I'm covered in wool and leather, but I've got a vision to execute, rain or shine.

"Jess, let's get a few more and adjust the light stand a little."

We go on shooting for another hour. I drag poor Jess to an alleyway and a farmer's market. I switch up my makeup because it looks too severe, then too soft. By noon, we start to pack up and clean.

I get home around four o'clock to relieve the nanny. Mad is out of town for work. Allie and Miles, our Great Danes, are waiting for me, tails thwacking against the door when my key hits the dead bolt. Allie's body wiggles furiously when I open up, and since she's too polite to jump, I duck down to her, rub the soft, thin skin of her ears, and let her hot tongue hit my cheek. Miles leans his already enormous body into me without a hint of civility. He's gentle but he sure is giant.

"I know, I know," I tell them in the sky-high excited voice that dogs like best, and I walk to the kitchen and send two cups of kibble tumbling into their dishes. I play puppets with Navy and watch her draw pictures of sunshines, all while trying to ignore the insistent pinging from my phone. I manage to make it through dinner, bath, and bedtime without emailing anyone. It's a miracle. When Navy stops stirring, I pour myself a hefty glass of Sauvignon Blanc.

For a collection of glorious seconds, while Allie curls up by my feet and the wine hits my temples, the day is over. I have nothing to do and nobody to answer to. But a few breaths later, my phone blinks and buzzes from the kitchen table and I'm back at work again. Somebody posted another comment.

"Gorgeous!"

"Love it!"

"Where are your pants from?"

"Tag your pants!"

"Looking good, Mama."

"🖤🖤🖤🖤"

"Must be nice."

"Yas."

I'm numb to all of it, but five minutes later, I'm trying to get a good picture of my wine to share.

The lamp in the living room isn't cooperating, so the wine and I move to the bedroom instead. I rest the glass on a pile of highly recommended books. I haven't even read the jackets yet, but everybody else is posting about them. I imagine I could write something relatable like "Wild Friday over here" or maybe something a little more nerdish, "Books and wine, my favorite way to spend a Friday." It isn't though. My actual favorite way to spend a Friday involves a long soak in the tub, shitty Mexican food delivered by Postmates, and a solid half-bottle of white. I could post it, but the things that are real people would never really believe.

"LOL yeah right," they'd write. "No way she eats that and looks like that."

I think about engagement and outsmarting the algorithm and decide that I should be *in* the picture with the wine. It's about nine-thirty now.

Quickly, I head to the bathroom to put on a little lipstick and slip into the nice silk pajamas that a partner brand sent over. I contemplate making myself a bubble bath, staging it with candles (sponsored) and a new lotion (also sponsored) and making a real thing of it, but don't. I posted a bubble bath picture in July, which wasn't that long ago. By the time I could get in, the water would be cold anyway.

The wine stares impatiently at me from the nightstand. I notice the pads of my fingers smudged on the glass and wipe it carefully with a Kleenex.

Allie and Miles are sprawled out on the bed groaning like they've been on their feet

all day. Based on the amount of hair on the duvet, though, I'm guessing they had a pretty casual Friday. Still committed to the wine photo, I fumble with my phone at the edge of the bed trying to take a one-handed selfie without slicing my forehead in half or giving myself seventeen chins. It's impossible. An iPhone camera could give Mount Rushmore extra chins.

"Shit!" I whisper-yell as the wine glass bonks against the lampshade and everything sloshes to the rim.

Allie grumbles, reminding me to watch my language, and I wish more than anything she had opposable thumbs.

"Do you want to be in the picture *with* Mom?" I ask her and Miles. People do love dog content, and who wouldn't? Miles lifts his great big dinosaur head at me and yawns. Allie hauls her body up and retreats to the sofa, which for her, is saying a lot.

I try a couple more times to get the perfect real, casual, carefree selfie that doesn't look too good or too bad, before finally giving up around 10 p.m. I have red lipstick on and I haven't left the house. I spent two hours trying to stage a picture of myself that didn't look staged. My stomach snarls at me. I forgot to eat my dinner. Again.

In the kitchen I make myself a Kashi and oat milk and try to forget about all of it. If I close my eyes, the little bran flakes sound like blowing leaves when they leave the box. If I take a deep breath, I can smell my special red Tom Ford candle. I untie the drawstring on my pants and sit alone at the table with my stomach rolling onto the tops of my thighs, knowing that this is the picture that people *should* see but never will: the woman who is never too tired to spruce up her feed but is always too tired to feed herself. It's messed up and I know it. Reflexively, I take pictures of what I'm wearing, eating, and doing. *What happens when documenting life becomes more important than living it?* What happens when we're staying so connected with one another that we forget how to connect with ourselves? How can we create anything of meaning if we don't make time and space for it? If all we want is more, more, more?

Allie comes back to me and lays her head in my lap, honey-brown eyes looking up at mine, doggy brows rising into perfect triangular peaks. Nearly a million people follow me online, but I scroll through the pretty pictures just like they do, wondering how people look like that, spend like that, and manage to do it all. Even more tragically, I wonder why I *can't*. I'm popular and privileged. I make my living on social media. If it's bad for me, it's worse for everyone else. The phone blinks at me once more. I put it on silent, turn it facedown, and smother it with a dish towel.

The next day I map out a few weeks of content with my assistant. We schedule another two brand campaigns, a sponsored makeup tutorial, and the fall fashion preview I nearly melted to create.

"The pictures turned out great!" my assistant announces proudly. "You look stunning!"

"I felt like garbage the entire time." I laugh.

She laughs too. "It doesn't matter. You look totally amazing."

If it doesn't matter, maybe it should.

What happens when joy is a picture on our phones instead of a feeling in our bones?

What if we're all just pretending?

I pull my hair into my signature messy bun, open my computer, and get to work.

Keep SAKES

Messy Bun

I promise, this is the only diet advice I'll ever give you: cut down on the phone stuff. Your mind, body, heart, kids, partner, pets, and plants will thank you. The past few years, I've reduced the noise drastically. I used to post four times a day, and now I post once a day, if that. The quality of the content is higher and the stress level is lower. Given the documentarianish nature of what I do, taking a break is not easy, but it's essential. I'm proud and privileged to be a part of people's daily lives, but once in a while I realize I'm absent from mine. Protect your time. Preserve your energy. Love your people. Here's what I do to get back to reality.

The Doable Digital Cleanse

THE 24-HOUR RULE

If something monumental happens, I sit on it for a full day before spilling the beans online. It gives me a chance to savor things and process them privately without any validation or vilification from others. Sometimes, I decide not to share at all.

THE 6 P.M. RULE

No phones after work. When my screen time is up, the second I open my front door, the phone gets stashed in a drawer and it stays there until morning.

THE 30-MINUTE RULE

Warning: this one is hard-core.

If you dare, sneak into your phone settings and set a hard limit for problematic apps. I could get sucked into Instagram all day. I know that because sometimes, I really do. On an iPhone, go to "Settings," find "Screen Time," then turn it on. Select "App Limits," then "Add Limit." Next, set the amount of time allowed. I try to stick to thirty minutes if I'm looking to cut down.

THE ONE-BOOK RULE

A digital detox isn't over until I have finished reading one full book from cover to cover. It doesn't need to be Tolstoy, just something worth cuddling up with and bringing along to coffee. It reminds me that every time I get lost in the scroll, I could be getting lost in a story. It helps that I live right down the road from one of planet Earth's best independent bookstores (I love you, Parnassus!).

THE ZERO-NOTIFICATIONS RULE

Taking a step back from tech isn't easy, and the fact that our phones beckon sweetly to us every few minutes doesn't help matters. When I turn off my notifications, I'm much less inclined to pick up my phone and get distracted.

Yummm!

Apps Are for Eating

Remember back when downloading an app meant crushing the Bloomin' Onion with your dad at Outback? Ahh, simpler times! While my tastes have become slightly more refined, I'm still a sucker for a good appetizer, and if I had my way, the entrée would be a thing of the past. Having people over for cocktails and tiny bites is my favorite way to celebrate. Here are some of my go-tos.

Mini Butternut Squash Tacos

These little guys are always a hit. We have friends who are vegan and friends who process their own venison, but everybody can agree on the butternut squash taco.

FOR THE SQUASH, YOU'LL NEED:

1 medium butternut squash, diced into one-inch cubes

2 tablespoons olive oil

1 teaspoon garlic powder

Salt

Pepper

FOR THE SLAW, YOU'LL NEED:

2 cups purple cabbage, julienned

2 cans black beans, rinsed and drained

1/3 cup green onions, chopped

1/3 cup fresh cilantro, chopped

2 to 3 tablespoons fresh lime juice

1 teaspoon olive oil

1/4 teaspoon salt

YOU'LL ALSO NEED:

8 street-sized flour tortillas (Mad loves flour tortillas)

Garnishes: cilantro, feta, avocado slices, roasted pepitas, guac, whatever you like

STEPS:

1. Preheat the oven to 400 degrees.

2. Toss squash in olive oil, garlic powder, salt, and pepper on a sheet pan.

3. In a large bowl, mix purple cabbage, black beans, green onions, cilantro, lime juice, olive oil, and salt and let rest. (I like it crunchy, but if you're looking for a little tenderness in life, you can mix this up earlier in the day and keep it covered in the fridge.)

4. Roast squash for 25 to 30 minutes until fork tender.

5. While the squash is cooking, warm your tortillas on both sides in a skillet over medium heat (about 30 seconds per side). Move them to a plate and cover with a dish towel to retain heat and moisture.

6. When the squash is done, assemble your tacos! Slaw first, then squash. Optional: garnish with feta, avocado slices, cilantro, and roasted pepitas!

Marinated, Warmed Olives

It doesn't get any fancier than a tricked-out bowl of olives, and honestly, I'm not entirely sure why. They're idiot-proof, but everybody gets starry-eyed when I bring them out. I like to serve them with grilled sourdough and whipped ricotta, but they can go in any direction you want.

YOU'LL NEED:

1 pound high-quality pitted olives

1/2 small fennel bulb, thinly sliced

2 to 3 cloves garlic, minced

1/3 cup olive oil

Zest of 1 orange, cut into strips

1/2 teaspoon fennel seeds

Pinch red pepper flakes (more than a pinch if you like your olives sassy)

Salt and pepper

(I like Castelvetrano, Kalamata, and Frescatrano, but any mix is great!)

STEPS:

1. Drain brine from olives.
2. Cook fennel, garlic, and olive oil over medium heat in a skillet until they begin to soften.
3. Add olives, orange zest, fennel seeds, and red pepper flakes, stirring to combine.
4. Lower heat to medium-low and cook for 3 to 4 minutes.
5. Let rest in the warm skillet for an additional 2 minutes.
6. Add salt and pepper to taste, if needed.
7. Serve in a bowl alongside your party faves.

Note: These can be made with unpitted olives and it's arguably even yummier, but I try to avoid situations where people have to spit into a cocktail napkin midconversation.

Eggplant Hummus

The saddest shade of brown, eggplant hummus may not be a showstopper, but it is a crowd-pleaser. Even when I get the "I just don't know about eggplant" spiel, the bowl is always empty at the end of the night (don't worry, I make extra and squirrel it away for lunches).

YOU'LL NEED:

1 large eggplant

1 15-ounce can chickpeas, drained and rinsed

1 teaspoon (or more!) cumin (I like roasting and grinding cumin seed because it's amazing and much stronger. If you go for it, start with ½ teaspoon and add more to taste.)

½ teaspoon smoked paprika, plus extra for topping

1½ tablespoons lemon juice

2 garlic cloves, grated

3 tablespoons tahini

Dash hot sauce

Salt and pepper to taste

3 tablespoons ice-cold water, if needed

STEPS:

1. Preheat oven to 425 degrees.
2. Poke eggplant all over with a fork and place on a parchment-lined baking sheet.
3. In a medium pot of water, bring chickpeas to a boil and simmer for 5 to 10 minutes. Drain and set aside. Cooking the chickpeas a little bit now makes for a nice, creamy consistency later.
4. Roast eggplant for 35 to 40 minutes until it caves in and looks terribly sad.
5. Place eggplant in a large mixing bowl (or the bowl of a blender—I use an immersion blender) with chickpeas, cumin, paprika, lemon juice, garlic, tahini, hot sauce, salt, and pepper. Blend or mix with hand mixer, adding cold water if needed, until desired consistency is reached.
6. Add additional hot sauce, salt, or pepper to taste, and garnish with smoked paprika.
7. Serve with pita and crudites.

Without further ado,
the hairdo that started it all

The Messy Bun, in All Her Glory

Without further ado, the hairdo that started it all:

1. First off, skip your daily wash and embrace the dirty hair. A messy bun looks its best with a little texture.
2. Pull your hair into a low ponytail and secure.
3. Add mousse to the lengths and work through, setting with a blow-dryer if needed and back-combing here and there to create volume and texture.
4. Wrap your pony around the base, pinning where needed and pulling looser in spots to create wonderfully messy dimension.
5. Tuck the ends under and secure with pins, the existing elastic, or a new elastic.
6. Pull a few strands loose to frame your gorgeous face.
7. Spray with your favorite product for extra hold and ta-da! Success!

CHAPTER 11

Nēmah

You can't give what you don't have.

The skin is hanging from my cheeks and I look ten years older than I did this morning. I thought I'd get a shower in, but there's no way. Our second child, five-month-old Indie, is in the bedroom crying out for the last of my milk. There isn't any left but he refuses to believe it. My body is done. My breasts are just empty, stretched-out flaps of skin. It doesn't matter how much water I drink or how many fenugreek capsules I take. At least three plastic baby bottles, and possibly a plate, clatter onto the floor downstairs in the kitchen. Mad says "*shit*" as quietly as possible and carries on mixing Indie's food.

Standing in the bathroom, I put the pajamas I was desperate to get out of, back on. They smell like night sweats and children's Tylenol. Both the kids are getting over RSV and all we can give them is acetaminophen and Popsicles. Nobody is sleeping and it shows. The pot light over top of me burns out with a sad flicker, bringing an extra shadow to my face. I remember when the bathroom was my sacred place. Now it's just a mirror smattered with Sensodyne, a heap of towels, and a toilet sitting in the corner with the lid up, like it's gasping for breath. Indie whimpers again and I abandon my shirt completely, rushing to the nursery in my bra.

"It's okay," I call out to him, but it isn't okay. I just want it to be.

The sound of my voice calms him when I reach the threshold. He knows nothing other than to trust and love me fully. I am his sacred space, milk or no milk. I turn on the light and his face scrunches up from the shock of it. Scooping him up, I tell him that he's the most handsome baby in the world and we go to the rocker where he can wake up slowly. My weight settles into the chair, his weight settles onto my chest, and for a moment there is nothing but the groan of leather and warm baby's breath in my ear.

"Ready!" Mad calls up.

Indie pushes his body away from mine and reaches for my face like I'm as much a miracle as he is. One year into a pandemic, political turmoil, losing jobs, losing our nanny, and losing hope, the fact babies still grab mothers' noses, cry out for milk, and smile when the window catches a beam of sun feels like the greatest comfort in the world.

"Hey," Mad says cautiously, meeting me when I'm halfway down the stairs. "I need you to look at this."

He hands me a bottle of thawed breast milk for Indie and we walk into the kitchen together.

There is an open cardboard box that says "Priority." Laying inside in a bed of bubble wrap are two generic tubes of lotion. They're all wrong. The color is off. The font is weird. The print is crooked, sloping lazily down the side. It looks like we don't care.

Mad lost his job when Covid hit, and ever since we've been working together on a skin care line for mothers and building the strong, supportive community that they deserve. I dreamed it up right after I had Navy, imagining what it would be and how it would make people feel. When Mad lost his job and the both of us stared into the murk of Indie's ultrasound photo, drinking in equal parts joy and fear, bracing for life to change again, we knew it was the perfect time for him to come on board. I needed someone who could lead operations, who understood me, and who would be a champion for new parents. Madison Lee is a champion for just about everyone.

The pregnancy with Indie was brutal compared to my first. I was sick for months. I had a toddler to chase. I had a business to run. The world fell apart. I was scared. I wanted to create what I needed, something that would give women life as they were nurturing

it. I wanted to create it now. We started talking to doctors and chemists immediately. I survived Zoom meetings on saltine crackers and Sprite, energized by the thought that we could empower women to make a proud, open choice to care for themselves . . . and by Navy frequently popping her electric-blonde head into the frame to say hello.

The skin care line would be simple, artistic, clean, and safe. It would have proven preventive ingredients *and* soul. It would be a chance for me to use my nursing background and for Mad to use his (maddeningly) brilliant ability to build a brand out of thin air. It would also be a ton of work.

There would be no rest, not even after the baby came, but I wanted to give women what I couldn't give myself. I wanted to build an inclusive community that embraced the complexities of motherhood with honesty, gentleness, and trust. For months, I slathered my belly in the stretch-mark cream formulas we were testing while baby Indie kicked and fluttered against my ribs. When he was born, I tried just about every treatment on my c-section scar. Eventually we landed on the ideal combinations, which was bound to happen since after nine months, I was basically a professional moisturizer.

"What do you want to do?" Mad asks, giving me a tired look from across the island, eyes darting past the stack of dirty dishes, the diapers that Navy pulled out one by one, and the groceries that had been delivered but that we hadn't had time to unpack.

"Scrap it. We have to. It isn't us," I mutter, shaking my head at the sad-looking containers. "It's sloppy."

Navy cackles from her seat, covered with pudding, staring at her tablet, completely mind blown by Daniel Tiger's comedic timing. A crushed juice box falls from the trash can and brings a dirty wipe along with it.

"Too sloppy?" he jokes. "You sure?" I ignore him. I'm too tired to be angry.

My phone releases an urgent succession of beeps and reminders.

"Call with Team Spain 2 hours"

"Photos HG in 30 minutes"

"Writing tomorrow"

"Tylenol Kids: Now"

"Mama!" Navy is up now, dancing in the hallway with her *Paw Patrol* underwear down around her ankles. "Potty!"

Indie yanks at my hair and proudly waves a few strands in the air. I hardly even feel it.

Mad lifts him from my arms and he cries, going bright pink in the face and suddenly remembering that his teeth are coming through. Navy starts to pee on herself, and *she* cries. Miles sees another dog outside and stamps his enormous paws on the concrete floors. It's all too much. I beg for the day to be over and longer at the very same time. Nobody is happy and nothing is done. Everybody wants something but there is little left to give.

Around 7 p.m. we put the kids in the tub to wash the avocado from their bellies and let Navy stretch bubbles between her hands like a big foaming accordion. With their joy bouncing from the tiles to the ceiling, the bathroom—even with its handprints on the wall and naked toilet-paper roll—is a sacred space again. Navy wiggles her body through her pretend cloudscape to where Indie is sitting and plants a kiss on his head, which he can hardly believe. His giggles are pure magic, nothing less. They fill the whole house and turn Mad and I to goo. In these perfect moments, nothing else matters. Nothing.

Mad had sorted out the packaging problem, relaying a series of dissatisfied messages that I didn't have the energy to deliver myself. There are four different teams working on the project in three different countries. We have a huge contract to fulfill and tight deadlines we're in danger of not meeting. We're supposed to launch in two months and we haven't even held the product yet. I swallow hard when I think about it and my chest tightens.

"Ne-mah, Ne-mah, Ne-mah," Navy sings, slapping the water with her little palm.

"Nemah" is what she calls me when she can't get "Mom" out. After agonizing over names for the line, "Nēmah" is where we landed. It means "God's gift" in Arabic. We heard her say it one night and it just clicked. When I googled it and discovered what it meant, we were goners. It was perfect.

Navy is grinning so big her eyes wrinkle, staring up at me with the same unshakable trust that Indie does. I rub a pink glob of shampoo onto her head, rubbing her little temples like she's at a spa day, and rinse her with a plastic bucket. We pretend that I'm a waterfall and she lets out a long sigh. Mad sighs too. We all do.

"Your turn," Navy smiles, grabbing the tiny bucket from my hand, scooping up the hazy bath water and pouring it onto my forearm. I can see the grime, soap scum, the bloated Cheerio, but I don't care.

"Nemah, Nemah, Nemah," she whispers, letting the water rush over me again and again, mothering me the very best way a two-year-old can.

The love, the softness, the connection between us, in even a single moment, really is God's gift. It's the core of the earth, the reason for being, the ultimate bliss. There is nothing like it. Indie coos at us and together we wash his back, listening to the bubbles as they snap-crackle into thin air.

After, tangles are wrestled and diapers are changed. Prayers for Daniel Tiger's health and happiness are sent out into the universe, and video monitors are repositioned. With a grunt, Navy pulls her body onto her new big-kid bed and tucks each of her stuffed animals in before slipping under the covers herself. Mad rocks Indie until his eyelids get heavy and his smile begins to quiver. I sneak in for a quick kiss before Mad sets him down into the crib and starts his favorite rainforest sounds. Why they chose to include the howler monkey, we'll never understand.

We head downstairs and get ready to tie up loose ends. Mad sends the West Coast emails while I get the dishes and empty the tub. As the last of the grey water swirls around the drain, I think about mothering and Nēmah and Navy James, pouring water again and again onto my thirsty skin.

The faucet drips slowly onto the porcelain basin.

You can't give what you don't have.

I turn it back on, shut the drain, and light a candle, dipping my ankles, then my whole body, into the water and letting it rise around me, making a proud, open choice to care for myself.

Keep
SAKES

Nēmah

There's a final straw out there for all of us, something that tips the scales from "enough" to "way too much." For me, it was two rather innocent-looking packaging prototypes. I've always been one to get through it, to put my head down and work, to push my limits. What I realized when surrounded by crying babies, a world on fire, an overflowing trash can, and a deadline I couldn't make, was that *I hadn't been pushing my limits, I'd been ignoring my boundaries.* And I'd been doing it for years. Caught up in the grind of mothering others, I forgot how to mother myself.

We all want to be successful, loved, and respected, but if we fail ourselves in the process, do we ever really get there? I don't think so.

Mama's had a day.

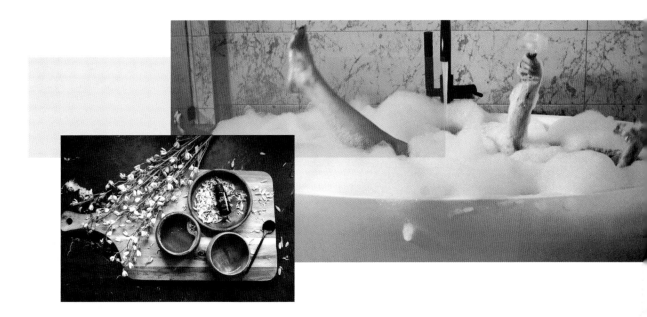

Type-A *Bubble Bath*

I'll never forget sweet Navy James setting aside her firm nightly rendezvous with Mr. Bubble to care for me instead. For a two-year-old, it was a pretty astounding show of empathy. For me, it was a major wake-up call. I was burning out and my kids were watching it happen.

Having a bath might seem kind of puny, but for me it was a radical act of self-love. It was modeling a choice I wanted my daughter, my friends, and my fellow parents to make. So at exactly 8:22 p.m. on the hardest, longest day of my life, I fed my reckless, insufferable type-A, Enneagram 3 energy into curating the ideal bubble bath. Now I do it every week, for me and also for Navy, because I know she's watching. Here are a few of my essentials for a watertight grown-woman bath time.

WHAT TO USE

Homespun soak! I would never hate on Mr. Bubble, but making a custom brew feels ultra-luxurious and takes less than five minutes. This basic blend is milky, moisturizing, vegan-friendly, and easy to personalize (but if you're looking for a mountain of suds, stick with Mr. B.).

YOU'LL NEED:

1 cup Dr. Bronner's Pure-Castile Soap (or another unscented fave)

2 to 3 tablespoons fractionated coconut oil

A few shakes of lavender, chamomile, or other essential oil of your choice. Since I'm normally trying to channel that chill koala bear energy, I go for eucalyptus.

Mix soap, coconut oil, and essential oils. Add a few ounces to the tub and store any leftovers in a plastic container or mason jar when you're all done!

WHAT TO DRINK

Sometimes a turmeric tea does the trick, but other times, Mama's had a day. Friends, let me introduce you to Mary's Bathtub Gin:

YOU'LL NEED:

1 ounce gin

2 to 3 ounces lime juice

A touch of soda

A splash of Jack Rudy Classic Tonic Syrup

A whole lot of ice (it gets` hot in there!)

WHAT TO LISTEN TO

The bubble bath is a perfectly acceptable place to zone out and get your Sigur Rós on, but for me, there are few things more restorative than a belly laugh. The three men always welcome in my tub are Jason Bateman, Sean Hayes, and Will Arnett. Download the *SmartLess* podcast; it doubles as an ab workout.

Be sure to keep that phone far out of reach—no scrolling, only soaking.

WHAT TO READ

Reading in the tub always feels a bit dangerous, but the risk of drowning your *Vogue*s diminishes greatly with a solid bath caddy. Lately my tub lit consists of old issues of *Porter*, anything by Glennon Doyle, and *World Travel: An Irreverent Guide* by Anthony Bourdain. As a rule, I keep it light.

WHAT TO EAT

Is it poor form to eat in the tub? Probably. But is it also the best? You bet! The key is handheld, minimal-mess snacks, so leave the hoagie and take the cannoli. If you're fresh out of cannoli, go for warm chocolate chip cookies.

LASTLY, DUCKS OR NO DUCKS?

Ducks. Always ducks.

Life Hacks for
the (Over) Working Mom

I'm of the belief that nearly all moms, whether employed outside the home or not, are working harder than just about anybody else. Mamas who do have the wherewithal to stay at home with the kids, I truly have no idea how you do it. I'm toast after a long week-end. Raising children, especially babies, requires an incredible amount of physical (and spiritual) energy, and finding the right balance feels impossible some-times . . . okay, most of the time. Here are a few things that help me steady the scales.

GO HANDS-FREE

Bluetooth and babywearing all day long! Indie lived in his wrap cuddled up on my chest for the first three months of his life, and it freed me up to do everything from my dishes to my taxes.

MEAL DELIVERY

Some mamas get real nerdy about meal prep; I am not one of those mamas. Not having to shop and chop saves me hours every week and I love not having to think about how much cilantro is too much. There are so many affordable, healthy options out there that plop ready-to-use ingredients right down on your stoop.

BRING YOUR BABY TO WORK OR BRING YOUR WORK TO BABY

With work-from-home the norm throughout the pandemic, your employer may be more flexible than you think. If you're expecting or planning to be, it might be worth discussing the options with HR. *Happily Grey* has always been a baby-friendly zone and I love having my kiddos as a part of the team.

ROUTINES AND THEN MORE ROUTINES

Everything is easier when everyone knows what to expect. Navy knows we do bath, then book, then bed every night. If for some reason I get stuck at work or on a call, our sitter can easily step in without throwing her off. The routines are just as important for me too. If I don't make "me time" a mandatory part of my day, it won't happen.

OUTSOURCE

You can't do it all, so don't. Look deep into your heart (and your budget) and think about what you can hand off to somebody else. Also, for my stay-at-home parents, you don't need to work forty hours a week to justify:

- having a nanny or willing family member,
- ordering food,
- needing a break,
- needing a therapist, or
- taking something off your very full plate!

0600 *Good morning*

One Day, Two Toddlers

"It'll be fun," we said.

"They'll be best friends!" we said.

It is and they are, but Mad and I were definitely a little starry-eyed and naive about having two children within two years. The early months were chaos, the middle months were chaos. The right now? It's chaos too. To those of you living off coffee and half-eaten applesauce pouches, picking up random wet diapers from the middle of your living room floor, secretly fantasizing about setting fire to the Mickey Mouse Clubhouse: you're doing great and you're not alone. Buckle up and take a look at our day.

0800 *Breakfast*

0900 *Park play*

1200 *Yumm*

1500

Play it out

"*The right now? It's chaos too.*"

1800 *Tub time*

2100

CHAPTER 12

Golden

I hope that they remember the beauty of not-knowing in a world that seems to have all the answers. I hope I remember it too.

The ride to the start line takes just twenty minutes from midtown Manhattan. We go from the public library along the East River, past Battery Park, and through the greyest parts of Brooklyn, which look extra grey when the leaves have died from the London plane trees and the sun is just hinting at daylight. The bus rolls slowly past a sweeper clearing the last of the trash and spent foliage, onto the Verrazzano-Narrows Bridge, where the Hudson drains into the Atlantic. We arrive on Staten Island with hours to spare and I wait, from 7 a.m. until noon, watching the sun stretch its long, lazy arms over the city skyline and settle into the day.

Today I am not Mary Lawless, or Mary Seng, or Mary Lee, or Mom, or an influencer, or a model, or a businesswoman. I am 33231, a runner, one of more than thirty thousand who come every year to climb the city like a mountain. And this year it's a special climb, the fiftieth anniversary of the race, a race that celebrates an iconic city and the incredible,

proud, diverse humans that make it what it is. We runners are diverse, too, a mix of Olympians and accountants and amputees and schoolteachers and grandpas and everything else a person could be. There's even a duck named Wrinkle who seems nervous and has red-webbed sneakers on his feet. All of us, different as we may be, have a reason to be here, to board the plane, get on the bus, and run twenty-six miles across five boroughs in a pandemic. I don't know their reasons, but I know mine, and at mile twenty-three your reason is all you have left.

I'm running for an organization called Every Mother Counts that promotes safe pregnancy and childbirth for women everywhere, particularly in the developing world where everything that hit us hard in 2020 hit them harder. I'm running for the mother who feels lost in her body and the one who loves it for the first time, for the mother who looks at her baby and feels everything and the one who feels nothing, for the mother who sleeps when the baby sleeps and the one who doesn't even know how to rest anymore. In the eight months since Indie was born, I have been all of them. And a few more. It has been a privilege to be allowed to feel, grieve, celebrate, and reflect after the birth of my children. It isn't a freedom afforded to everyone. As I trained, sprained, sweat, and hammered the feeling from my thighs, I thought of freedom above all else. That's what running is to me. I'm running for women everywhere, but also for me.

"You're taking on too much," my friends would say. "You'll be overwhelmed."

But running was my refusal to be overwhelmed. It was waking up and claiming a part of the day as my own. It was doing one thing at a time instead of forty, being alone—blissfully alone—on a carless, soulless, desolate street. It was a return to thirteen years old, stretching my legs as far and as fast as they could go at the cross-country meet, around the bases at softball, toward home. It was success and failure with only God, the feral cats, and myself called to witness. There was no internet blast (not most of the time anyway), no affirmation or defamation; I was just a person doing a thing that mattered to them.

I would start my training runs from home, waking before the babies, leaving the dogs and Mad in a big velvety coma on the bed. I'd put on an outfit that nobody would see or like or pin and step out into the low-lying fog that visits our neighborhood when the seasons begin to change. The world would stand still and say almost nothing. The chatter of automatic sprinklers might travel across the green lawns to my ears, or a cricket may stay out past bedtime, but otherwise it was silence, starlight, and absolute perfection. At the end of our walkway I'd stop to stretch, something I didn't need to do at twenty-four but must do a decade later. I'd listen for the awful, wonderful crunch of vertebraes L1 through L5 as I touched my toes, grasping for the rubber tread under for thirty seconds and wincing. Then I'd hook my palm around the front of my shoe at the laces, bend my knee, and pull back, until heat swelled in my quad and melted away. Last, two quick jumps, three big breaths, and off toward the city.

I never took the time to choose a route. I'm not sure why, but I'd ended up traveling back along the roads that led me here to Mad and the babies, to home and to trusting myself. We live just two miles from Golf Club Lane, the skinny little street where the old townhouse sits, hopefully with its hamburger carpet and lazy brown fans still intact. That's where I'd start off, running a ten-minute mile past Lipscomb University to warm up the tiny muscles that protect my ankles.

The house is still there exactly as it was, tan and happy, but the young tree wised up and has taken more of the sky for itself, stretching up tall to the power lines and dwarfing the facade with its big brash leaves. I remember walking in the front door for the first time, my arm in his, feeling hope and wondering if Nashville would make everything better, if a new place would be enough to shush the soft voice that showed up on my wedding day and never really stopped speaking to me. I remember leaving the house for the last time, too, also hopeful, carrying forward the things I took from the life we were trying to build and bringing them on to the life that awaited me. With the sun making pink in the sky, I'd give it all a good look, a loving look, and move on, turning onto Belmont Boulevard and then down Music Row, a crowd of tiny craftsman homes where most of country music unfolds.

Around mile five I'd pass the old bar with the plastic skeletons where I fell in love with Madison Lee just from the sound of his voice. In the early morning, if it weren't for the cigarettes speckled on the sidewalk, the little house could be a law office or day care center. I remember what it was to walk toward him, guided only by fascination and hope. I remember what it was to see him and know him and adore him in an instant, the same quiet, measured voice that told me not to get married at twenty-two now screaming over the music, begging me to dive straight into his arms. I remember what it was to listen to myself. I could stare at the bar for days, reliving and rejoicing, but I move on.

An hour or so in and the birds are awake, mostly swifts and little finches. I'd pick up the pace a bit, turning right again onto Broadway where a few cars might whoosh past and disappear over the big, calf-melting hill. I'd run down farther, and farther, toward the river, where the cleaning crews had normally already begun pressure washing the sticky, battered floors of honky-tonks. I'd look down at my arm and find "always m" staring up at me, throbbing along with my heartbeat—crooked, messy, wonderful. When the road turns to river, I'd turn around and head home, passing the tall grey tops of the hospital where I held my babies and where the nurses—cheerful when they needed to be, assertive when they needed to be—held me.

For the last five miles, I'd disappear into the percussion of my thick rubber shoes on the tarmac and the breath slipping through my teeth, reliving old dreams, imagining new ones, feeling nothing but gratitude for the vastness of the world and the will to explore it.

Today, with the brine of the harbor in my nose and Brooklyn in the corner of my eye, there is nothing familiar and I'm electrified by it. I breathe the cool, smelly city deep into my chest and wish that all mothers, all women, all people, would feel so wonderfully, wildly free.

I stand alone in the grey shadow of Fort Wadsworth and wait for hours that go by like instants. Many of the other runners are first-timers like me, getting ready for the crack of the gun, the surge of adrenaline, the run we've been training for. I tug at the corners of my orange bib, smooth my number with the flat of my palm, and watch clouds of my breath scatter into the sky. I stretch and I jump and I hydrate until finally, fizzing and popping, the loudspeaker calls our corral. Collectively, we shake the cold from our legs and line up behind the fast-fluttering blue flags just before noon. I quickly check the video Mad and Navy made for me to watch before I started.

"I luw you. Run your race. I so proud of you," she says with her face pressed right up next to her daddy's.

The cannon that starts us off is loud, but we are louder, filled with optimism at mile one and cheering without a hint of shame for ourselves. I step onto the stark, sun-bleached bridge, leaving behind the banks of porta-potties and big white tents, the shaking cow-bells and screaming of the start village. Quickly though, I lose myself in the sound of two thousand footsteps, in the bright-colored clothing, the smells of freshly applied Speed Stick, and the pulsing blades of the NYPD helicopters that follow us in the sky. It is all brand-new to me.

When we spill out into what I think is called Bay Ridge, the crowd is waiting for us with outstretched hands. Children who were out on their walks, and just happen to stumble upon us, jog alongside, stuffed into their puffy winter coats, dispensing high fives and telling us "Go! Go! Go!" Their parents, who are almost exclusively in the wrong shoes, do all they can to keep up past the bone-colored townhomes, parkettes, and convenience stores. Bike horns and cowbells begin around mile eight and Brooklyn becomes the block party I hoped it would be. There's old-school hip-hop playing and high fives and somebody holding a sign that says, "Run Now, Wine Later."

Don't worry. I smile at her. *It's already chilling in the fridge.*

I'm thinking about everything: the past month, the past year, the living that came before today and the living that will come after.

As I cross the Pulaski Bridge with its big red beams into Queens, my knees begin to ache, and I miss my family after half a day. Navy and Indie don't leave my mind. I picture her toddling around Central Park, watching the people run in their colorful flurry, probably more interested in the broad fall leaves and sidewalk pennies, longing for the ducks in the pond and a ride on the carousel. Indie will be in his fleece looking like a shrunken yeti and laughing at her, laughing at everything the way only Indie does. He can find joy in the dryer lint, in the eyelash on his sister's cheeks, in limp green beans, and in his own head cold.

I want them to have everything in life but nothing more than what they have right now: wide-open eyes; brave, loving hearts; hunger pains for the start of the next day. The older they get, the more they'll know, and the less they'll wonder. The more work it will be to find magic in a sunburst through an overcast sky or the duck casually floating on the pond. I hope that every answer they learn brings a new question, that as they grow up they know that they never have to stop growing. I hope that they remember the beauty of not-knowing in a world that seems to have all the answers. I hope I remember it too.

The short trip into the Bronx should be drama free, but a shock of lactic acid turns my muscles to glue around mile twenty. My breath gets slower but my heart speeds up. I'm a full minute slower than my goal time and it's way past time to eat. I jog slowly and squeeze a pack of almond butter into my mouth. It's like swallowing concrete.

"Go, Mama, go!" somebody yells, probably not to me, but I receive it anyway and quietly repeat it as a mantra.

Go, Mama, go.

Go, Mama, go.

Go, Mama, go.

Nothing is steep but everything is uphill, and my joints begin to complain about the incline and the cold weather and the impact. I see a shop or a salon or restaurant or something named "Breathe" and I receive that too. It makes everything better. I don't shut out the pain, I don't abandon my body; I just breathe through the aches, the cramps, the nerves that ebb and flow, and the adrenaline of the crowd. I'm barely moving, but still, *Go, Mama, go.*

At mile twenty-three, the boughs of Central Park come into view and I stop to throw up on my shoes. I feel terrible, but it doesn't faze me. I'm expecting it in the same way somebody doing ayahuasca might expect to vomit and have a deep conversation with Mother Mary. I wipe the sour from my mouth, look up, and take it all in: the runners' faces, which are sullen and have been drained of their expressions, the lights of the empty NYPD cars swirling around and getting lost in the blue of the sky, the American elms that even in my adulthood still beg me to climb them. *Go, Mama, go.* I wobble back onto the course and haul my legs onward in long, exaggerated strides that feel like heaven, stretching out my calves one step at a time. The breeze I needed hits me and I can think only of Navy.

I picture her clapping wildly with no idea why, picking out the colors from the outfits she sees like they're rare birds and wondering why she gets to be so tall today on Mad's shoulders. Indie won't remember. If he remembers anything from this age it will be being told over and over that he's handsome. He won't remember, but Navy might. This could be a snapshot of childhood, a hallowed place she returns to when she's a woman yearning for a feeling she may not have but can recall in vivid color behind closed eyelids and smiling lips. She may remember looking over the crowd with cold, pink cheeks, seeing thousands of happy strangers, and then, among them, her mother. I pick up my pace, throw it all in, and begin sprinting the final stretch, a flat stretch of asphalt flanked by a hundred billowing flags from around the world and the most beautiful crowd of people I've seen in my life.

In the beautiful crowd I see *my* beautiful people: my mom holding Indie, bouncing him up and down and yelling, "Go, Mary, go!" and Navy, as predicted, on Mad's shoulders. My daughter and I lock eyes and her entire face lights up with love and sunshine. Extending her pudgy little finger, she starts yelling, repeating everything that Mad yells—including a few overexcited things she probably shouldn't. My body fills with the warmth of family and I go faster and faster. *Almost there.*

I hear breath and a set of rubber soles scraping the pavement. A man about fifty is running beside me and our feet find the wide yellow finish line. We collapse into an embrace, claiming and sharing our victory.

"We did it!" Both of us are cheering and both of us are in tears.

My breath slows and the adrenaline heating my chest becomes rapture, not for finishing but for allowing myself to begin, for choosing the life that nobody expected, a life too complex and rich and scary and wonderful for anyone to have dreamed for me. With my chest heaving, I grab a blue poncho and a Gatorade, neither of which do anything to quiet my violent post-race shakes, and a brown-haired woman with a headset hands me a weighty medal on a blue-and-white ribbon. I head straight for my family.

Navy is pointing at a snail when I see her, eyes bluer than blue and big as coat buttons. I hear her voice, which sings like a song even when she's talking to a bug on the ground. Mad smiles, Indie smiles even bigger. Navy lifts her head from the glistening slug, waits a moment, and comes careening toward me. Though my still-quaking muscles hate me for it, I squat deep and hold her, drinking in the fresh air that she is, burying my head in the crook of her shoulder. I pull away from her for just a moment and transfer the medal from my neck to hers. She looks down, touches it nervously at first, then finds her face reflected in the luster and grins. I don't know if she'll remember it, but I will.

Keep
SAKES

Golden

I felt a lot as a child, maybe more than most. I played but I also planned. I wondered but I worried too. It's not that I didn't enjoy childhood; I dressed up in costumes and fished in the pond and ran wild through the fields. But I also asked big questions, and those big questions were hard on my little heart.

What does it all mean?

What happens when you grow up?

I want to make everyone happy. How do I make everyone happy?

When you grow up, is happiness harder to find?

With smiling, tan-legged dolls scattered all over my floor, I thought often of the future, plotting it out in little vignettes with plastic people and things. First she will go to school, then she will meet her husband. They will move into a big pink house

With smiling, tan-legged dolls scattered all over my floor, I thought often of the future, plotting it out in little vignettes with plastic people and things.

and have lots and lots of pink babies. They will work hard and make good choices. God will reward them because that's how God operates.

Out the window, as golden fields surged like ocean waves and dust blew up shimmering from the ground, the world called to me. But all I could think about was growing up. What would I do? Who would I love? Where would I live? How would I get there? When?

I forgot to ask why the dirt was sparkling or how the long stalks of sorghum grass didn't snap when the wind forced them over.

I grew up. I got married. I achieved all my goals and missed nearly everything else. It was all just black and white.

I've spent most of my adult life learning all over again how to play, dream, and discover. It's been hard work, but I've had wonderful teachers. Navy, who reminds me to chase bubbles, find artwork in the clouds, let my hair get wild and tangled. Indie, who is the world's foremost expert in belly laughter and loving avocado. At thirty-four years old, I am the youngest, freest, and most at peace I have ever been, and though there are lines at the corners of my mouth and a few coarse greys on the top of my head, I am just beginning. The more love I give to my inner child, the more love I give to my children, the more love they give to themselves.

Mantras for Mondays (and Tuesdays, and Wednesdays . . .)

I am right.
I am wrong.
I am good.
I am learning.

I set a lot of reminders for myself but they're mostly about Zoom meetings and switching the laundry over so that our house doesn't fill with the smell of wet death. I'm not great at mindfulness, and in a time of spiritual crisis, I'm much more likely to caffeinate than meditate. At the end of the day when the work is done, the babies are down, the emails are answered, the dogs are walked, the sex (I mean, maybe) is had, I don't have loads and loads of emotional bandwidth to connect with sister moon and brother sun or whoever it is the kids are communing with these days.

So, like I do with the stinky laundry and the Zooms, I set my intention, and then I set my reminder. This is what my week of mindfulness looks like.

Monday **EYES OPEN WIDE.**

Setting an intention feels extra important at the beginning of the week, and for me it's a good time to recommit to curiosity and awareness, not focusing so hard on one thing that I miss everything else.

Tuesday **I'M DOING ENOUGH. I HAVE ENOUGH. I AM ENOUGH.**

Chances are, by Tuesday I'm doing a little too much already. I need a reminder to slow down and step back.

Wednesday **BE.**

I'm so bad at staying present, I had to write it on my body. Midweek mayhem is real, the urge to disassociate is real. Coming back home to the here and now is almost always the right choice for me, even if I need a little help to get there.

Thursday **THANKFUL, THANKFUL, THANKFUL.**

There are people who do Taco Tuesday and people who do Thankful Thursday. There are people who do both (I am one of those people).

Friday **I AM RIGHT. I AM WRONG. I AM GOOD. I AM LEARNING.**

My job here is to learn, not to know. If I've made mistakes during my week (which by Friday, I absolutely have), I take a moment to give myself grace.

Saturday **WE BELONG TOGETHER.**

Because it's easy to forget that, when Navy is coloring on the walls, Indie is gassy, and Mad takes the last cup of coffee.

Sunday **IT IS SAFE TO REST.**

It is not only safe but necessary.

Love Letters

When Indie was six months old, I checked into an emotional wellness center about an hour outside Nashville called Onsite. After three years of listening to friends' testimonies, I committed to a five-day Living Centered program. I'm proud of making the decision to go, proud to share it here, and deeply privileged to have had the resources available to me when I needed them. And I really did need them. I had hit the proverbial wall and instead of taking it as a sign, I told myself to put my back into it, work harder and longer, hustle and don't give up. Well, I gave out instead. I had a lot of recovering to do and no idea where to begin, so I spent five days at a very green farm feeling things, healing things, and reconnecting with myself.

Of all the exercises they gave us (and there were a lot), the one that brought me the most peace was writing a letter to my inner child, putting it in the mail, and sitting down weeks later in complete stillness to read it. Anybody can do this anytime, and you can use the blank page to say whatever you need to. It's brought me so much peace and joy that I've basically made it into a new-age Christmas tradition. In December, my three closest friends and I get together for a holiday lunch, take some time to write our letters (before the festive negronis happen, of course), and afterward, one of us has the job (the honor, really) of mailing them out. If you haven't reached out to your five-year-old self in a minute, she's probably missing you. And I promise, she's absolutely worth keeping in touch with.

Dear Younger Self,

SLOW DOWN. PAUSE. BE PATIENT. REST.

You are an ambitious girl in an ambitious world, determined, always trying to stay a few steps ahead. People love that about you. I love that about you. But don't forget to just be. Make curiosity your greatest ambition. Stay present. Savor your dreams as hard as you chase them and never let tomorrow's shadow keep you from standing in today's light. God has so much in store for you. Let him pull off a few surprises, okay?

The world isn't all black and white, which I know is both a relief and a total nightmare. You don't know everything. You can't control everything. Not everyone loves Whataburger and Jesus. You have so, so much to learn, and you're going to get it wrong sometimes (probably a lot), but don't be afraid. This learning will be the greatest thrill of your life. Nobody will tell you this out loud, but the richest people on earth are the ones with the questions, not the ones with the answers. Keep asking questions.

Belonging will feel hard sometimes. You fit in this world just perfectly, like birds in the big sky, but it won't always seem that way. When this happens, I need you to do something brave. I need you to love yourself. Look at yourself with joy and fascination, just like you do the rest of the world. Explore, feel, wonder, because you are not all black and white either. Cry, belly laugh, grieve, hope, yell, whisper, get mad, get silly, love yourself. Fail, succeed, mourn, celebrate, begin things, end them, evolve, love yourself. The day you love yourself is the day you stop proving yourself to others. It's a really, really, really good day.

I see you. I love you. I hear you. Keep your eyes wide open and I promise your heart will follow.

xx

M

Heirlooms

In November, New York City seems to fill with the hope for snow. The shop windows dress early with evergreens, nutcrackers, and working toy trains. Bursts of holiday music escape the open doors of Starbucks and Macy's. On the brightest, bluest days, you find yourself praying for a sky that's somber and slate colored. Even when it's forty-five degrees out, you look up, longing for a miracle to tumble down slow and land on the ends of your lashes.

Navy spent most of our trip to the most magnificent city on earth staring up at the sky, waiting, wrapped up in the possibilities hidden within the puffy, thistledown clouds. I found myself doing the same. Together, imagination carried us off, goose bumps pricked our arms, and we stood, mother and daughter, marveling at our world. I wanted to remember it and stay connected to it forever. When you travel somewhere special, with someone special, you pick up a keepsake.

I tried to find something in the city that captured the sense of wonder just perfectly, but I couldn't. So when we got home, I scoured the internet. I wanted a piece of jewelry that would honor my inner child, something that would remind me to nurture her and hold her close. I wanted something that would remind me to stare up at the sky every so often and imagine, just like Navy does. Most of all, I wanted something that I could pass on to her one day, telling her about the secretly beautifully grey New York afternoon that was perfect to nobody else but us. My greatest hope is that as my daughter grows and changes and becomes, she stays connected to the magic in her world. As we get older, it is so easy to forget that it's right there, all around us. Nothing is more magical than a mushroom.

Mushrooms make me happy. I've been drawn to them ever since I was a little girl. They're beautiful, complex, ever-changing, healing, nourishing, enduring, and mind expanding (not for me, but, hey, medicinal properties are medicinal properties). They grow, even in the dark, and on the surface you can see only a fraction of their beauty. Most of it lies underneath. Something about them just feels safe and welcoming to me, and I love that these two mushrooms are connected, little Mary and me, today. At first glance it may look like the big mushroom is protecting the tiny one, but really, I think it's the other way around.

As you travel, the sky will be an endless blue, a brooding shadow, and every color that stands between them, every iteration of misery and joy. Some days you won't notice it and other days, for no explicable reason, it will be glorious to you. Remember those moments, carry them forward, share them with the ones you love, *commemorate them*. Keep your eyes open wide.

Keep your eyes open wide.

Acknowledgments

I would like to thank each of you for showing up, supporting, and sharing this journey with me. You have allowed me the space to create, to grow, and to open my eyes a little wider. For that I'm forever grateful.

Shannon, you are an angel from above. One of the kindest, wittiest, and most beautiful souls I know. You have played a leading role in artfully and delicately bringing these stories to life. This book would absolutely not be possible without your support, love, and never-ending guidance.

To my mom and dad (Pam and Sam) and my siblings (John, Amy, and Stephanie): Thank you for the unconditional love and the experiences and lessons that shaped me. These memories I cherish most.

To Allie, my four-legged best friend who has been by my side through it all: Our connection is its own, your loyalty is resolute, and our love is boundless. Everyone thinks they have the best dog, but I know the truth in that. I love you, Allie girl.

Most of all, I want to thank my best friend and soulmate: my husband, Madison. I am deeply thankful for the unwavering support and love. This journey has been everything I could have hoped for and more. To our children, Indie and Navy: You are the greatest joy. Thank you for the color you bring to my life.

Photo Credits

Unless otherwise noted below, photographs of the people and places depicted in this book are from the personal archives of Mary Lawless Lee.

- **Chayse Carmichael:** front endsheets (Mary on beach; Mary in black Polaroid), back endsheets (wineglass), 28, 38, 50–52, 102 (left), 120, 156–57, 180–81, 184 (top), 194, back endsheets (Mary on beach; Mary's pants)
- **Mary Craven Photography:** 80
- **Emily Dorio:** 66–67, 108–9, 174–75 (background), 175 (right), 176–77
- **John Hillin:** 119, 146, 164–65
- **Cibelle Levi:** 166
- **Emmy Lowe:** 56 (right)
- **MarathonFoto / Gameface Media:** 188, 191 (top right)
- **Sophia Matinazad:** front endsheets (Mary in field), back endsheets (Mary holding Navy)
- **Jessica Steddom:** front endsheets (Mary fishing, Mary in sunflowers, Mary in white dress) 4, 5 (left), 10–18, 22, 25, 30 (left), 35–36, 42, 49, 54 (bottom), 70, 76, 82–84, 88, 90 (bottom), 92, 94, 96 (right), 98, 104, 107, 110, 115, 117, 122–24, 126 (top right and bottom), 131, 133–37, 139, 141–42, 143 (top), 144, 152–53, 158, 160–62, 169–70, 173, 175 (left), 178–79, 184 (top), 191 (top left and bottom left), 198
- **Kt Sura:** back endsheets (Mary with Navy on shoulders), 26–27, 30 (right), 54 (top left and right), 58, 64, 69, 77, 96 (left)
- **Emily Travis:** 68 (scrubs sketches)
- **Unsplash:** front endsheets (London street scenes, door, tiger, field, clouds, leaves), back endsheets (leaves, cows, chair with large windows, clouds, building on lower right)

About the Author

Mary Lawless Lee is a mother, writer, entrepreneur, and digital media personality dedicated to living creatively, chasing curiosity, and exploring the world through the lens of fashion, family, travel, and design. What began in 2012 as a complement to her busy job as an ICU nurse quickly became a career of its own. *Happily Grey*, her now-iconic fashion and lifestyle blog, amassed a following of over two million and serves as a loving space for readers to connect with Mary's stories and their own, journeying together through life's highs, lows, and in-betweens. A proud Nashvillian, Mary lives with her husband, Madison; her children, Navy and Indie; and her Great Danes, Allie and Miles. Together, they run the Happily Grey boutique and Nēmah, a self-care and skin care line for mothers.

darling, you're different

I loved the until I met

drea

CURIOSITY IS A GOOD LEADER

What happens when documenting life becomes more important than living it